American Theatrical Periodicals, 1798-1967

American Theatrical Periodicals, 1798-1967

A bibliographical guide

Carl J. Stratman, C.S.V.

Duke University Press
Durham, N.C.
1 9 7 0

© 1970, Duke University Press
L.C.C. card no. 72-110577
I.S.B.N. 0-8223-0228-4
Printed in the United States of
America by the Seeman Printery

Preface

Arundell Esdaile, in *A Student's Manual of Bibliography*, defines a "Preface" as "useful for the author's afterthoughts, for first aid to reviewers, and for those acknowledgments to helpers which can so easily be overdone." I would like to use this Preface, not as an afterthought, but primarily as a place of prominence to call upon the assistance of all those who may have occasion to use the work and who have any information about American theatrical periodicals.

Although this bibliography lists some 685 theatrical periodicals, published in 122 cities and in 31 states, 85 of the periodicals have not been located in any library. Further, although 137 libraries are listed as containing one or more periodicals, 171 periodicals are incomplete, that is, without all issues having been located.

Thus, much work still remains to be done before a complete bibliography of American theatrical periodicals becomes a reality. The present work is a preliminary and tentative effort in that direction, a beginning. That it may one day be as complete and accurate as possible may I call upon all scholars who have any information regarding unlocated titles, complete runs of a work, or knowledge of any errors, to forward such information to me—for use in a second edition—or to have the material published in one of the journals devoted to the American theater.

In my research work I have visited fifty-one libraries in the United States. To the librarians of these institutions I owe a deep debt of gratitude for the kind assistance which they accorded me, and I would like to acknowledge that debt at this time. The libraries so visited are: Boston Public Library, Brown University, Catholic University of America, Chicago Historical Society, Chicago Public Library, University of Chicago, Cincinnati Public Library, Columbia University, De Paul University, Detroit Public Library, Folger Shakespeare Library, Fordham University, Free Library of Philadelphia, Hartford Public Library, Harvard University, Library of Congress, Loyola University of Chicago, Michigan State University, Minneapolis Public Library, New Haven Public Library, New York Historical Society, New York Public Library, New York University, Newberry Library, Northwestern University, Ohio State University, Pierpont Morgan Library, Princeton University, Rutgers University, St. Louis Public Library, St. Louis University, State University of Iowa, University of Cincinnati, University of Colorado, University of Delaware, University of Denver, University of Illinois, University of Kansas, University of Kentucky, University of Michigan, University of

Minnesota, University of Missouri, University of Nebraska, University of Notre Dame, University of Pennsylvania, University of Wisconsin, University of Wyoming, Washington, D.C., Public Library, Washington University, Wayne State University, and Yale University.

I would also like to thank Kenneth H. Cherry of the Duke University Press for his editorial advice and for his preparation of the chart of publication spans at the end of the book.

Contents

Introduction

One important area of the American theater which has been neglected in historical studies of theatrical activity is the American theatrical periodical, whose pages are the "abstract and brief chronicles" of the passing show. One obvious reason for such neglect is that no one, heretofore, has undertaken the preliminary step of gathering together and publishing the titles and locations of the hundreds of American dramatic periodicals upon which such a study would be based.

That such a work has long been needed may be sufficient justification for the appearance of this bibliography, in spite of any deficiencies which may be present. The following pages bring together for the first time some 685 American theatrical periodicals, published in 122 cities, and in 31 states, with locations of issues noted in 137 libraries.

A first step in the task of gathering titles was to make an examination of all available printed sources, such as the *Union List of Serials* and *New Serial Titles*, to establish complete titles, dates of first issues as well as the final ones, and frequency of publication. In addition, it was necessary to determine which of the periodicals with such seemingly dramatical titles as *Harlequin*, *Play*, and *Comedy* were actually devoted to the theater. For example, *Best Plays of the Year* (1962–), which is concerned with football and not Broadway successes, is naturally omitted.

A second step used in compiling the bibliography was to visit as many libraries as possible, in order to obtain the complete titles, sub-titles, editors' names, publishers' addresses, variations in runs, frequency of publication, as well as information concerning such matters as change of title. Over the years I have visited fifty-one libraries in the United States; of these very few had more than a half dozen theater periodicals, and these half dozen were frequently the standard ones, such as *Theatre Arts*, *Drama*, or various issues of *Variety*.

A third step adopted in the attempt to locate theatrical periodicals was to write several hundred letters to various libraries throughout the country with inquiries about specific titles. Often the letters brought negative responses from the ever courteous librarians, but occasionally a reply was in the affirmative, and another entry was noted.

Before discussing the format of the bibliography a few words may be in order in regard to the title, *American Theatrical Periodicals*, so as to avoid the possibility of any confusion concerning the limitations of the work. By the word "periodical" is meant all serials, from dailies to annuals, as well as directories, that are issued periodically. Newspapers are included when they are devoted primarily to some theatrical topic, e.g., *Variety*. The word "theatrical" is used to include periodicals which include the word "stage," "theater," or "drama" in the title or subtitle, or periodicals primarily devoted to: actors and acting; amateur and community theater; box office; dance and ballet; folklore music and acting; magic; music, when touching upon the stage in some manner; musical comedy; Negroes in the theater; opera; puppetry; repertory theater; theater management; vaudeville. The bibliography will not contain periodicals primarily devoted to: movies or the cinema, unless the periodical also covers the stage; television; radio; photography; literary periodicals which may, at times, carry a dramatic column.

Relative to the format of the bibiliography a chronological arrangement by year of first publication is adhered to from beginning to end. Within each year the periodicals are arranged in alphabetical order. Each entry includes, as far as possible, the following information:

1. The original title of the periodical.
2. The editor, or editors, when known.
3. The city of publication.
4. The publisher and the address, when known.
5. The number of volumes and issues, when known.
6. The dates of the first and last issues, when known.
7. Subsequent changes in title, if any.
8. Frequency of publication.
9. Miscellaneous notes as needed.
10. Symbols for libraries owning the periodical.

Titles

The titles and subtitles of periodicals are given as they appear on the title page. At times periodicals contain some descriptive or humorous information on the title page which is also included. For example:

The Cynick. By Growler Gruff, esq., *pseud.* Aided by a Confederacy of Lettered Dogs. Philadelphia, Pennsylvania. Vol. 1. Nos. 1-12. 21 September–12 December 1811. Weekly.

Editors

Whenever the editor's name appears either on the title page or somewhere in the periodical the name is given as it stands, immediately following the title of the periodical. If the name does not appear in the periodical, but is known, it is placed in brackets immediately following the title of the periodical. If the editor changes during the course of publication, and if the information is available, the date for each editor is placed in parentheses immediately following his name. For example:

The Arcadian. Edited by G. H. Butler (1875); L. Engel (to 1877); J.
  W. Tooley (1877–1878). New York, New York: 89 Nassau Street.
  Vols. 1-8, No. 2. 18 September 1872–12 January 1878. Weekly.

Publication information

Publication information, when it appears, is given. That is, the city
of publication, the publisher or printer, and the address are indicated as
they appear in the periodical, whether the information is on the title
page or elsewhere in the periodical. Whenever possible I have attempted
to retain the material on the title page as it appears. As a result, in
several cases, there may appear to be some inconsistency.

Volumes and issues

The number of volumes and issues, if they appear in the periodical,
are given immediately following the city of publication and the publisher. In a number of instances the issues are not numbered consecu-
tively, from the first to the last issue. When such is the case, and when I
have been able to determine the exact number of issues, I have inserted
this information in brackets. This approach has been taken, on the as-
sumption that more rather than less information is of value. The following
example may indicate what I mean.

Porter's Spirit of the Times. A Chronicle of the Turf, Field Sports, Literature and the Stage. Edited by W. T. Porter and George Wilkes.
  New York, New York. Vols. 1-11, No. 11. [Nos. 1-271.] 6 September
  1856–2 November 1861. Weekly.

Dates

Following the indication of the number of volumes and issues the
complete date is given for the first and last issue. For example the dates
"6 September 1856–2 November 1861" indicate that publication began
on 6 September 1856 and terminated on 2 November 1861. Because
most of the periodicals do not indicate their terminal date it is possible
that some of them may have more issues than are actually indicated. If
the periodical is still published this fact is indicated, after the initial
date is given, by the use of a dash. For example, an entry which reads
"September 1957–." indicates that the periodical is still published.

Frequency of publication

When known, the frequency of publication is given immediately
following the publication dates for the periodical. When there is any

variation from this frequency it is indicated by the use of parentheses immediately after the frequency is given. Further, when there is a stated change in publication frequency this fact is indicated. The following example indicates the form followed.

Music Trade Review. Edited by J. C. Freund. New York, New York. Vols. 1-10, No. 5. 3 November 1875–18 October 1879. Then, *Musical Times and Music Trade Review.* Vol. 10, No. 6–Vol. 11, No. 11. November 1879–10 January 1880. Semimonthly (3 November 1875– 18 October 1878); weekly (2 November 1878–10 January 1880).

Thus, the periodical was published in semimonthly form from 3 November 1875 to 18 October 1878. It was published in weekly form from 2 November 1878 to 10 January 1880.

Library holdings

For information regarding the holdings of specific periodicals in designated libraries I am dependent upon the following: (1) personal consultation of a library's holdings, based either on checking each issue of the periodical or on a check of the card catalogue; (2) letters from librarians; (3) information given in such works as the *Union List of Serials* and *New Serial Titles.* Naturally the last two works are the basis for the holdings of most libraries.

When no one library possesses all issues of a periodical, an attempt is made to locate enough libraries that a combination of these institutions will give a complete run. At times, however, when it has been impossible to locate complete runs of a magazine I have attempted to indicate the specific holdings of each library.

The holdings of the various libraries listed are represented by symbols. These symbols appear immediately after the numbered periodical entries. When a complete set of the periodical is not possessed by a library the actual holdings are specified by volume. In some cases, however, dates are used rather than volume numbers. At such times my information comes either from the listings in the *Union List of Serials, New Serial Titles,* from a letter from a librarian, or from the card catalogue of the particular library. This accounts for any lack of uniformity.

The actual format used is that which appears in the *Union List of Serials* and in the card catalogues of a number of libraries. Because the format is not immediately evident or self explanatory to the user, some examples, with explanation, may serve to obviate any difficulties. Parentheses follow each library symbol except when the holdings of the library are complete. Brackets are used within the parentheses to indicate which volumes are incomplete.

Sample entry 1

Boston Weekly Magazine. Devoted to Polite Literature, Useful Science, Biography, and Dramatic Criticism. Boston, Massachusetts: Tileson and Parmentier. Vols. 1-3. 12 October 1816–8 May 1819. Then, *Weekly Magazine and Ladies Miscellany.* New Series. Vol. 1. Nos. 1-41. 20 March–25 December 1824. Weekly. DLC, MB (1-3), MBAt (1-[3]), MH (2; New Series, No. [1]), MWA, NN ([1-2]), NhD ([1-2]-3)

DLC (Library of Congress) has a complete set of the periodical.

MB (Boston Public Library) has volumes 1-3 of the first series complete. It has no other volumes.

MBAt (Boston Athenaeum) has volumes 1 and 2 complete, and volume 3 incomplete, of the first series. It has no other volumes.

MH (Harvard University) has volume 2 of the first series, and the first issue, which is not numbered, of the New Series. It has no other volumes.

MWA (American Antiquarian Society) has a complete set of the periodical.

NN (New York Public Library) has volumes 1-2 of the first series, but both volumes are incomplete.

NhD (Dartmouth College) has volumes 1-2 incomplete, and volume 3 complete, of the first series. It has no other volumes.

Sample entry 2

Spirit of the Times. A Chronicle of the Turf, Agriculture, Field Sports, Literature and the Stage. New York, New York. Vols. 1-31, No. 20. 10 December 1831–22 June 1861. Weekly. CtY ([1], 9-[27]-[30]), MWA ([1-2, 5]-28, [30]), NR (1-10, [16]-[19]-31), PPiU (7-21)

CtY (Yale University) has volumes 1, 9-30. Of these volumes 1, 27, and 30 are incomplete.

MWA (American Antiquarian Society) has volumes 1-2, 5-28, 30. Of these volumes 1-2, 5, and 30 are incomplete.

NR (Rochester Public Library) has volumes 1-10, 16-31. Of these volumes 16 and 19 are incomplete.

PPiU (University of Pittsburgh) has volumes 7-21, all complete.

Sample entry 3

New York Clipper. New York, New York. Vols. 1-72, No. 23. 1853–12 July 1924. Weekly. CtY ([7-11]-[13-15]-[17]-[19-20], [28-33]-[35-37], [39]-[44-49], [51]-[54]-[59]-[61]-[63-65]), DLC (4, 24, [26-28], 70-72), MH (14-64, 1866-1917), NN (4-72, 1856-1924)

CtY (Yale University) has volumes 7-20, 28-37, 39-49, 51-65. Of these the following volumes are incomplete: 7-11, 13-15, 17, 19-20, 28-33, 35-37, 39, 44-49, 51, 54, 59, 61, and 63-65.

DLC (Library of Congress) has volumes 4, 24, 26-28, 70-72. Of these volumes 26-28 are incomplete.

MH (Harvard University) has volumes 14-64. Harvard University indicates that these volumes are complete for the years 1866-1917.

NN (New York Public Library) has volumes 7-72. The New York Public Library indicates that these volumes are complete for the years 1856-1924.

Sample entry 4

La Lorgnette. Revue des Théâtres, Courrier des Salons, Journal des Artistes. Edited by L. Placide Canonge; James Foulhouze (beginning 23 February 1843). New Orleans, Louisiana: Imprimée par J. L. Sollée, Passage de la Bourse. Vols. 1-3. Nos. 1-31. 12 December 1841–20 April 1843. Semiweekly. LNHT (11 December 1842, January–2 April 1843, 9-20 April 1843), MB (12 December 1841–17 March 1842)

LNHT (Howard-Tilton Memorial Library of Tulane University) does not list its holdings for this periodical by volume and issue. It simply indicates that it has issues of the periodical for 11 December 1842, for January to 2 April 1843, and for 9–20 April 1843.

MB (Boston Public Library) does not list its holdings for this periodical by volume and issue. It simply indicates that it has issues of the periodical for 12 December 1841 to 17 March 1842.

Sample entry 5

Coward-McCann Contemporary Drama. New York, New York: Coward-McCann, 210 Madison Avenue. No. 1–. 1960–. Irregular. DLC (selective basis), MH (selective basis), MdBJ (selective basis)

The dashes which follow the first issue, and which also follow the date, serve to indicate that the magazine is still being published. The words "selective basis" after each library symbol state that these libraries have indicated that they keep the periodical on a selective basis only, that is, they keep only the issues which they wish to remain in their collection.

Sample entry 6

Playbill. A Weekly Magazine for Theatregoers. New York, New York. Vol. 1–. September 1957–. Weekly. CU ([3]–), IaU (1–), NjP (8–)

CU (University of California, Berkeley) begins its holdings with volume three, which is incomplete. It has all issues after that.

IaU (State University of Iowa) has all volumes, beginning with volume one.

NjP (Princeton University) begins its holdings with volume eight. It has all issues after that.

Brackets

Brackets are used extensively throughout this work, primarily in the following cases: (1) To indicate the name of a publisher, if the name does not appear in the periodical but is known. (2) To indicate the name of an editor, if the name does not appear in the periodical but is known. (3) To indicate the number of volumes or issues, if they do not appear in the periodical but are known. (4) To indicate dates which are uncertain. (5) To cite the specific authorities for certain titles of periodicals which are included but which have not been located. For example, the *Bulletin of Bibliography* is such an authority cited for indicating the existence of certain periodicals which I have not been able to locate. (6) To supply notes or information on various matters which have to do with the periodical. These notes generally follow the indication of frequency of publication. (7) To indicate which periodicals are on microfilm. (8) To indicate which volumes are incomplete in specific libraries.

Index

Finally, because an index is an important feature of any bibliography, an explanation of the present one may be in order. The entries follow a single alphabetical arrangement, embracing not only names of individuals, organizations, cities, and titles of periodicals, but numerals also. For example, the title *17th and 18th Century Theatre Research* is entered as if the spelling were "Seventeenth and Eighteenth." Information for each listing in the index is complete with entry number so that even for cross references there is no necessity to consult the cross reference itself. Included in the index are:

1. The titles of all periodicals, in italics, with the year (in parentheses) that the magazine began publication, and the entry number, as in

> *Scene* (1938), 431

2. Simple subtitles, followed by the word "See" and the title of the first issue of the periodical, together with the year it began publication and the entry number. The form is:

> *Actor's Regalio.* See *The-atrical Budget* (1823),
> 13

3. The names of editors. Following the name of the editor is the title of the periodical and the year it began publication, as well as the entry number. The form is:

> Sayler, Oliver M. (*Foot-light and Lamplight*, 1924), 319

4. All changes of title, followed by the word "See" and the title of the first issue, together with the year it began publication and the entry number. The form is:

> *Little Theatre Magazine.*
> See *Olympian* (1930), 369

5. Cities of publication or printing, followed by the title of each periodical printed in the city, and the year the magazine began publication, as well as the entry number. The form is:

> San Francisco, California.
> See *Actor* (1938), 419;
> *Daily Critic* (1867), 47

6. Universities sponsoring magazines, followed by the title of each periodical, together with the year it began publication, and the entry number. The form is:

> Stanford University. See
> *Bulletin of the Drama-tists' Assembly* (1938), 420; *Asides* (1940), 453

7. Theater organizations or groups, followed by the title of each periodical sponsored, and the year each began publication, as well as the entry number. The form is:

> Shakespeare Society of
> New York. See *New Shakespeareana* (1902), 155; *Shakespeariana* (1883), 91

8. Various terms such as "amateur," "ballet," "Catholic," "community," "dance," "magic," "music," "Negro," "opera," "puppet," "repertory," "Shakespeare," "Soviet," followed by the titles of all such magazines, and the year each began publication, as well as the entry number. The form is:

> Opera. See *Aria* (1935), 398; *Central Opera Ser-vice Bulletin* (1954), 555

9. Periodicals devoted to specific figures, such as Gilbert and Sullivan, Shakespeare, and Shaw. The form is:

> Shaw, George B. (*Califor-*
> *nia Shavian,* 1960), 622;
> (*Independent Shavian,*
> 1962), 648

10. Where the same title applies to a number of periodicals, the title is repeated in a chronological arrangement, and the date of original publication, and the entry number is indicated.

> *Curtain Call* (1937), 415
> *Curtain Call* (1944), 488
> *Curtain Call* (1946), 500
> *Curtain Call* (1961), 636

In the attempt to make the index complete, I have listed the title and entry number in as many different places in the index as is warranted by cross references. For example, the *Dunster Drama Review* was edited by Lance Morrow, Travis J. Williams, and Mark Coleman, sponsored by Harvard University, and published in Cambridge, Massachusetts. In the index the title, date, and entry number appear under: (1) Title; (2) Morrow; (3) Williams; (4) Coleman; (5) Cambridge, Massachusetts; (6) Harvard University.

Library Symbols*

AU University of Alabama, University, Alabama
ArU University of Arkansas, Fayetteville, Arkansas
AzU University of Arizona, Tucson, Arizona
BM British Museum, London, England
C California State Library, Sacramento, California
C-S California State Library, Sutro Branch, San Francisco, California
CL Los Angeles Public Library, Los Angeles, California
CLSU University of Southern California, Los Angeles, California
CLU University of California at Los Angeles, Los Angeles, California
CSmH Henry E. Huntington Library, San Marino, California
CSt Stanford College Libraries, Stanford, California
CU University of California, Berkeley, California
CU-B University of California, Bancroft Library, Berkeley, California
CaAEU University of Alberta, Edmonton, Alberta, Canada
CaOTP Toronto Public Library, Toronto, Ontario, Canada
CoD Denver Public Library, Denver, Colorado
CoDU University of Denver, Denver, Colorado
CoFS Colorado State University, Fort Collins, Colorado
CoU University of Colorado, Boulder, Colorado
CtW Wesleyan University, Middletown, Connecticut
CtY Yale University Library, New Haven, Connecticut
DFo Folger Shakespeare Library, Washington, D.C.
DGU Georgetown University Library, Washington, D.C.
DLC Library of Congress, Washington, D.C.
DeU University of Delaware, Newark, Delaware
FMU University of Miami, Coral Gables, Florida
FU University of Florida, Gainesville, Florida
GEU Emory University, Atlanta, Georgia
GU University of Georgia, Athens, Georgia
IC Chicago Public Library, Chicago, Illinois
ICA Art Institute of Chicago, Chicago, Illinois
ICHi Chicago Historical Society, Chicago, Illinois
ICL Loyola University, Chicago, Illinois
ICN Newberry Library, Chicago, Illinois
ICU University of Chicago, Chicago, Illinois
IEN Northwestern University, Evanston, Illinois

*The symbols for American libraries are based on *Symbols Used in the National Union Catalog of the Library of Congress* (9th ed. rev.; Washington, D.C., 1965).

IU University of Illinois, Urbana, Illinois
IaU State University of Iowa, Iowa City, Iowa
IdU University of Idaho, Moscow, Idaho
InU Indiana University, Bloomington, Indiana
KAS St. Benedict's College, Atchison, Kansas
KU University of Kansas, Lawrence, Kansas
KyU University of Kentucky, Lexington, Kentucky
LNHT Howard-Tilton Memorial Library of Tulane University, New
  Orleans, Louisiana
LNSM St. Mary's Dominican College, New Orleans, Louisiana
LU Louisiana State University, Baton Rouge, Louisiana
LU-M Louisiana State University, Medical Library, New Orleans, Lou-
  isiana
MA Amherst College, Amherst, Massachusetts
MB Boston Public Library, Boston, Massachusetts
MBAt Boston Athenaeum, Boston, Massachusetts
MBtS St. John's Seminary, Brighton, Massachusetts
MH Harvard University, Cambridge, Massachusetts
MMeT Tufts University, Medford, Massachusetts
MWA American Antiquarian Society, Worchester, Massachusetts
MWelC Wellesley College, Wellesley, Massachusetts
MdBE Enoch Pratt Library, Baltimore, Maryland
MdBJ Johns Hopkins University, Baltimore, Maryland
MeB Bowdoin College, Brunswick, Maine
MeU University of Maine, Orono, Maine
MiD Detroit Public Library, Detroit, Michigan
MiDW Wayne State University, Detroit, Michigan
MiU University of Michigan, Ann Arbor, Michigan
MnHi Minnesota Historical Society, St. Paul, Minnesota
MnM Minneapolis Public Library, Minneapolis, Minnesota
MnS St. Paul Public Library, St. Paul, Minnesota
MnU University of Minnesota, Minneapolis, Minnesota
MoK Kansas City Public Library, Kansas City, Missouri
MoS St. Louis Public Library, St. Louis, Missouri
MoSU St. Louis University, St. Louis, Missouri
MoU University of Missouri, Columbia, Missouri
N New York State Library, Albany, New York
NB Brooklyn Public Library, Brooklyn, New York
NBuG Grosvenor Reference Division, Buffalo and Erie County Public
  Library, Buffalo, New York
NBuU University of Buffalo, Buffalo, New York
NFQC Queens College Library, Flushing, New York

NHi New York Historical Society, New York, New York
NIC Cornell University, Ithaca, New York
NN New York Public Library, New York, New York
NNC Columbia University, New York, New York
NNCoCi College of the City of New York, New York, New York
NNF Fordham University, New York, New York
NNJ Jewish Theological Seminary of America, New York, New York
NNMM Metropolitan Museum of Art Library, New York, New York
NNQ Queens Borough Public Library, New York, New York
NNR Russell Sage Foundation, College of the City of New York, New York, New York
NNS New York Society Library, New York, New York
NNU New York University Libraries, New York, New York
NPV Vassar College, Poughkeepsie, New York
NR Rochester Public Library, Rochester, New York
NRU University of Rochester, Rochester, New York
NbU University of Nebraska, Lincoln, Nebraska
NcD Duke University, Durham, North Carolina
NcGW University of North Carolina at Greensboro, Greensboro, North Carolina
NcU University of North Carolina, Chapel Hill, North Carolina
NhD Dartmouth College, Hanover, New Hampshire
NhU University of New Hampshire, Durham, New Hampshire
NjP Princeton University, Princeton, New Jersey
NjR Rutgers University, New Brunswick, New Jersey
NjT Trenton Free Library, Trenton, New Jersey
NmU University of New Mexico, Albuquerque, New Mexico
NvU University of Nevada, Reno, Nevada
OC Public Library of Cincinnati and Hamilton County, Cincinnati, Ohio
OCU University of Cincinnati, Cincinnati, Ohio
OCl Cleveland Public Library, Cleveland, Ohio
OClW Western Reserve University, Cleveland, Ohio
OT Toledo Public Library, Toledo, Ohio
OU Ohio State University, Columbus, Ohio
OkS Oklahoma State University, Stillwater, Oklahoma
OkU University of Oklahoma, Norman, Oklahoma
OrU University of Oregon, Eugene, Oregon
PBL Lehigh University, Bethlehem, Pennsylvania
PEa Easton Public Library, Easton, Pennsylvania
PHi Historical Society of Pennsylvania, Philadelphia, Pennsylvania
PP Free Library of Philadelphia, Philadelphia, Pennsylvania
PPL Library Company of Philadelphia, Philadelphia, Pennsylvania
PPi Carnegie Library of Pittsburgh, Pittsburgh, Pennsylvania

PPiCI Carnegie Institute of Technology, Pittsburgh, Pennsylvania
PPiD Duquesne University, Pittsburgh, Pennsylvania
PPiU University of Pittsburgh, Pittsburgh, Pennsylvania
PSC Swarthmore College, Rosemont, Pennsylvania
PSt Pennsylvania State University, University Park, Pennsylvania
PU University of Pennsylvania, Philadelphia, Pennsylvania
RPB Brown University, Providence, Rhode Island
RU University of Rhode Island, Kingston, Rhode Island
SdU State University of South Dakota, Vermillion, South Dakota
T Tennessee State Library, Nashville, Tennessee
TN Nashville Public Library, Nashville, Tennessee
TxDA Dallas Public Library, Dallas, Texas
TxDaM Southern Methodist University, Dallas, Texas
TxU University of Texas, Austin, Texas
USl Salt Lake City Public Library, Salt Lake City, Utah
ViRU University of Richmond, Richmond, Virginia (VRU)
ViU University of Virginia, Charlottesville, Virginia (VU)
ViW College of William and Mary, Williamsburg, Virginia (VW)
WHi State Historical Society of Wisconsin, Madison, Wisconsin
WM Milwaukee Public Library, Milwaukee, Wisconsin
WU University of Wisconsin, Madison, Wisconsin
WaS Seattle Public Library, Seattle, Washington
WaU University of Washington, Seattle, Washington
WvU West Virginia University, Morgantown, West Virginia
WyU University of Wyoming, Laramie, Wyoming

American Theatrical Periodicals, 1798-1967

1798

1. *The Thespian Oracle.* Or Monthly Mirror, Consisting of Original Pieces and Selections from Performances of Merit, Relating Chiefly to the Most Admired Dramatic Compositions, and Interspersed with Theatrical Anecdotes. Philadelphia, Pennsylvania: Printed for T. B. Freeman, No. 39 South Front Street. Vol. 1, No. 1. January 1798. Monthly. [Also on microfilm.] ICN, MB, MH, PHi

1805

2. *The Theatrical Censor.* By a Citizen. Philadelphia, Pennsylvania: John Phillips, at his Circulating Library, South Fourth Street. Nos. 1-17. 9 December 1805–3 March 1806. Irregular. [At the end of No. 8 is an announcement that future numbers will be issued weekly at No. 42 Walnut Street as well as at John Phillips' Circulating Library. The dating which appears on the cover does not always conform to that which is within the issue. Nos. 15 and 16 are dated March 15 and 17. No. 16, for Wednesday evening, March 19, on pp. 145-146 treats *The Gamester*, yet No. 17 is supposed to be March 3.] CSmH, DFo, DLC, MB, MWA, NIC, PHi

3. *The Thespian Mirror.* A Periodical Publication Comprising a Collection of Dramatic Biography, Theatrical Criticism, Miscellaneous Literature, Poetry, &c. &c. Edited by John H. Payne. New York, New York: Printed by Southwick & Hardcastle. Vol. 1, Nos. 1-14. 28 December 1805–31 May 1806. Weekly. [Frank L. Mott's *A History of American Magazines* (Cambridge, Massachusetts: Harvard University Press, 1930-1957), gives the last issue as 22 March 1806 (I, 166). Seemingly he did not know about the later issues. Also on microfilm.] CtY (missing No. 14), DLC (missing No. 14), MH, NN

1806

4. *Theatrical Censor and Critical Miscellany.* By Gregory Gryphon, Esq. Philadelphia, Pennsylvania: J. Phillips. Nos. 1-13. 27 September–20 December 1806. Weekly. [Five numbers were published in New York. Mott dates the final issue December 1806.] MBAt, N, NIC, NN

1809

5. *The Rambler's Magazine and New York Theatrical Register.* For the Season of 1809–10. New York, New York: Published by D. Longworth, at The Shakespeare-Gallery, 11 Park. Vols. 1-2, No. 1. 1809–1810. [Nos. 1-4.] CSmH, DLC, ICU, (missing Vol. 2), IU, MB (Vol. 1), MH, NIC, NN, OCl, PU

6. *The Thespian Monitor.* And Dramatick Miscellany. By Barnaby Bangor, Esq. Philadelphia, Pennsylvania: Published by Mathew Carey, No. 122

Market Street. Vol. 1, Nos. 1-4. 25 November–16 December 1809. Weekly. [Also on microfilm.] CSmH, DLC, MB, MH, NN (incomplete)

1810

7. *The Mirror of Taste and Dramatic Censor.* Edited by Stephen Cullen Carpenter. Philadelphia, Pennsylvania: Published by Bradford and Inskeep; New York, New York: Inskeep and Bradford; Boston, Massachusetts: William M'Ilhenny. Vols. 1-4, No. 6. January 1810–December 1811. Monthly. [A drama was appended to each number of Vols. 1-2.] CtY, DLC, ICN, ICU, LU, MB, MH, MWA, MdBE, MnU, NIC, NN, NRU, NjP, PEa, PHi, PP, PU, RPB, TxU

1811

8. *Baltimore Repertory of Papers on Literary and Other Topics.* Including a Selection of English Dramas. Baltimore, Maryland. Vol. 1, Nos. 1-6. January–June 1911. Monthly. DGS, MdBJ, MH, MWA, NN, PHi

9. *The Comet.* By Walter Wildfire, *pseud.* [Edited by Joseph Tinker Buckingham.] Boston, Massachusetts. Nos. [1]-13. 19 October 1811–11 January 1812. Weekly. DLC, MB, MH, MWA, MeU

10. *The Cynick.* By Growler Gruff, esq., *pseud.* Aided by a Confederacy of Lettered Dogs. Philadelphia, Pennsylvania. Vol. 1, Nos. 1-12. 21 September–12 December 1811. Weekly. [The principal purpose of the periodical was to censure theatrical managers in the city for abolishing old theater boxes.] CSmH, CtY, DLC, IU, MB, MnU (missing No. 3), MH, NIC, OU, PPL

1814

11. *Whim.* Philadelphia, Pennsylvania. Nos. 1-10. 14 May–16 July 1814. Weekly. MH (Nos. 1-3), PHi. (Nos. 1-10)

1816

12. *Boston Weekly Magazine.* Devoted to Polite Literature, Useful Science, Biography, and Dramatic Criticism. Boston, Massachusetts: Tileson and Parmentier. Vols. 1-3. 12 October 1816–8 May 1819. Then, *Weekly Magazine and Ladies Miscellany.* New Series. Vol. 1, Nos. 1-41. 20 March–25 December 1824. Weekly. [Merged into *Boston Spectator,* 1825.] DLC, MB (1-3), MBAt (1-[3]), MH (2; New Series, No. [1]), MWA, NN ([1-2]), NhD ([1-2]-3)

1823

13. *The Theatrical Budget.* Or, Actor's Regalio; Being an Excellent Collection of Recitations, &c. New York, New York: E. M. Murden. Nos.

1-11. 1823. New Series. Nos. 1-13. 1828. Biweekly. [Caption title of the New Series, No. 1: *Elton's Theatrical Budget. Or Actor's Regalio.*] MH (Nos. 1, 8, 10-11; New Series, Nos. 1-6), NBuG (Nos. 1-6), NN (New Series, No. 13), NjR (New Series, Nos. 2, 12)

1824

14. *Theatrical Register.* New York, New York. 20 November and 11 December 1824. Weekly. [I have not been able to locate any other issues of this periodical.] MH

1828

15. *The Critic.* A Weekly Review of Literature, Fine Arts, and the Drama. Edited by William Leggett. New York, New York: Published at the Office of the Critic, 27 Wall-Street. Vols. 1-2, No. 7. 1 November 1828–20 June 1829. Weekly. [Missing the week of 28 February 1829, for which no pages are provided. There are no divisions or breaks for issues. Merged into *New York Mirror. A Weekly Gazette of Literature and the Fine Arts.*] CSmH, DLC (to 2 May 1829), ICN, ICU (to 2 May 1829), MB (to 2 May 1829), NN, NNS, PU, WHi

16. *Theatrical Censor and Musical Review.* Philadelphia, Pennsylvania: [Neal and Mackenzie]. Nos. 1-28. 1 October–29 November 1828. Daily (1–3 October); three times a week (4 October–29 November). DLC, MB, MH (21 October–13 November)

1829

17. *The Dramatic Mirror.* Containing Critical Remarks upon the Theatrical Performances of Every Night, in the City of Boston—with Bills of the Play. Boston, Massachusetts. Nos. 1-36. 24 January–19 March 1829. Daily (except Sundays and Mondays). MB, MH

18. *The Dramatic Mirror.* Containing Critical Remarks upon the Theatrical Performances of Every Night, in the City of Boston—with Bills of the Play. Boston, Massachusetts: Published Daily at the Printing Office of John H. Eastburn, No. 60 Congress Street. Nos. 1-56. 14 September–8 December 1829. Five days a week. [There is no title page. This may be a second series, following the preceding entry. See No. 13, 10 October 1829, p. 2. There are two issues numbered 33. Clippings are inserted in the Boston Library copy. See No. 13, p. 2.] MB

1830

19. *The Euterpeiad.* An Album of Music, Poetry, and Prose. Edited by C. Dingley. New York, New York: G. W. Bleeker. Vol. 1, Nos. 1-12. 15 April–1 October 1830. Then, *The Euterpeiad.* A Musical Review and

Tablet of the Fine Arts. Edited by J. Robinson (15 July–1 November 1831). New Series. Vol. 2, Nos. 1-13. 15 October–1 November 1831. Biweekly. MB, MH, NN, PPi, RPB, ViU

1831

20. *Spirit of the Times.* A Chronicle of the Turf, Agriculture, Field Sports, Literature and the Stage. New York, New York. Vols. 1-31, No. 20. 10 December 1831–22 June 1861. Weekly. [United with *Traveller*, 1832?–1834, as *Traveller and Spirit of the Times.*] CtY ([1], 9-[27]-[30]), MWA ([1-2, 5]-28, [30]), NR (1-10, [16]-[19]-31), PPiU (7-21)

1833

21. *Figaro.* A Petit Journal Devoted to Criticisms and Notices Concerning the Drama and Its Professors. Edited by W. Hart. New York, New York. Vol. 1, Nos. 1-10. 18 November–2 December 1833. Semiweekly. [The subtitle varies. No. 7 is dated 25 December 1833.] MH (1-10), NIC (Nos. 1-5, 7-10), NN (incomplete)

1834

22. *Entr'acte.* New Orleans, Louisiana. Vol. 1, Nos. 1-18. 9 February–13 April 1834. Semiweekly. LNHT

1835

23. *Gentleman's Vade-Mecum.* Or, The Sporting and Dramatic Companion. Philadelphia, Pennsylvania. Vols. 1-2, Nos. 1-78. 1 January 1835–25 June 1836. Weekly ICU ([1]), PPL ([2])

1839 (See *The Corsair*, Addenda, p. 86.)

1841

24. *The Dramatic Mirror, and Literary Companion.* Devoted to the Stage and Fine Arts. Edited by James Rees. New York, New York, and Philadelphia, Pennsylvania: Turner & Fisher. Vols. 1-2, No. 11. 14 August 1841–7 May 1842. Weekly. CSmH, DLC, ICU, MB (1-[2]), MH (1-[2]), NJP (1-[2]), PHi

1843 (See *The Anglo American*, Addenda, p. 86.)

25. *La Lorgnette.* Revue des Théâtres, Courrier des Salons, Journal des Artistes. Edited by L. Placide Canonge; James Foulhouze (beginning 23 February 1843). New Orleans, Louisiana: Imprimée par J. L. Sollée, Passage de la Bourse. Vols. 1-3, Nos. 1-31. 12 December 1841–20

April 1843. Semiweekly. LNHT (December 11 1842; January–2 April 1843; 9–20 April 1843), MB (12 December 1841–17 March 1842).

1847

26. *Broadway Journal and Stranger's Guide.* New York, New York. Vol. 1, Nos. 1-6. 3 July–7 August 1847. Weekly. NHi (1-2), NN (5-6)

1850

27. *L'Entr'acte.* New Orleans, Louisiana: Published by A. Britsch, with L. Placide Canonge. Vol. 1, Nos. 1-38. 5 December 1850–4 March 1851. Published three time a week. [See Max L. Griffin, "A Bibliography of New Orleans Magazines," *Louisiana Historical Quarterly*, XVIII (July 1935), 511.]

28. *Figaro.* Or, Corbyn's Chronicle of Amusements. A Weekly Journal, Devoted to Literature, Art, Music, and the Drama. Edited by Wardle Corbyn and J. W. S. Howe. New York, New York: W. Corbyn. Vols. 1-2, No. 23. 31 August 1850–10 May 1851. Weekly. [The numbering is irregular. Vol. 1, as Nos. 1-18; Vol. 2, No. 1, as No. 19. The subtitle varies.] DLC (Vol. 1, Nos. 1-19), MH (Vol. 1, Nos. 1-18), NN (Vols. 1-2, Nos. 4, 10-23)

29. *The Lorgnette.* Or Studies of the Town, by an Opera Goer. [Edited by Donald G. Mitchell.] New York, New York. Vol. 1, Nos. 1-24. 20 January–9 October 1850. Weekly (irregular). MH, MWA

30. *Prompter.* A Weekly Miscellany, Devoted to Public Amusements. Edited by Cornelius Mathews. New York, New York: W. Taylor & Co. Nos. 1-4. 1 June–5 August 1850. Biweekly (irregular). [Superseded by *The Prompter's Whistle.*] CtY, DLC, MB, MH, NN

31. *The Prompter's Whistle.* A Weekly Miscellany, Devoted to Public Amusements. Edited by "The Man Behind the Curtain." New York, New York: S. French. Nos. 1-4. 31 August–28 September 1850. Weekly. [Catalogue of the Brown Collection calls it a continuation of the *Prompter*, 1 June–5 August 1850.] CtY, DLC, ICN, MB, MH, NN (3 issues)

1853

32. *New York Clipper.* New York, New York. Vols. 1-72, No. 23. 1853–12 July 1924. Weekly. [Absorbed by *Variety*, 19 July 1924. Various subtitles: American Sporting and Theatrical Journal; The Oldest American Sporting and Theatrical Journal; and The Oldest American Theatrical Journal.] CtY ([7-11]-[13-15]-[17]-[19-20], [28-33]-[35-37], [39]-[44-49], [51]-[54]-[59]-[61]-[63-65]), DLC (4, 24, [26-28], 70-72), MH (14-64, 1866–1917), NN (4-72, 1856–1924). *Variety* has a complete file.

1854

33. *The Interlude.* New York, New York. Vol. 1, No. 1. 18 September 1854. [Playbill for the New York Theatre? No more published.] NHi

1856

34. *La Loge d'Opera.* (The Opera Box). Edited by Edward Clifton Wharton (English section); Charles de la Bretonne (French section). New Orleans, Louisiana. Vol. 1, Nos. 1-26. 15 November 1856–9 May 1857. Weekly. [Gertrude C. Gilmer, *Checklist of Southern Periodicals to 1861* (Boston, 1934), p. 37.]

35. *Porter's Spirit of the Times.* A Chronicle of the Turf, Field, Sports, Literature and the Stage. Edited by W. T. Porter and George Wilkes. New York, New York. Vols. 1-11, No. 11. [Nos. 1-271.] 6 September 1856– 2 November 1861. Weekly. [Merged into *Wilkes' Spirit of the Times*, and later, *Spirit of the Times and Sportsman.*] DLC (1-7), ICN (1-6), ICU (1-5), MiDU (1-5), MWA (1, [7, 9]), NIC (1-6), OC (1-[8])

1858

36. *Young's Spirit of South and Central America.* A Chronicle of the Turf, Field, Sports, Literature, and the Stage. Nashville, Tennesee; Louisville, Kentucky. No. 1. 17 April 1858. [Gilmer, p. 65.]

1859

37. *The Lorgnette.* Philadelphia, Pennsylvania: U.S. Steam-power Printing Office. Issued by Messrs. Wheatley & Clarke, Managers of the Arch Street Theatre. Vol. 1, [Nos. 1-69]. 14 April 1859–7/8 January 1861. Irregular. DLC (1859–[1861]), PU (1859–1861)

38. *Wilkes' Spirit of the Times.* A Chronicle of Turf, Field, Sports, Literature, and the Stage. Edited by George Wilkes (September 1859–October 1875); E. A. Buck (November 1875–16 September 1893). New York, New York. Vols. 1-18, No. 19. September 1859–June 1868. Then, *Spirit of the Times.* A Chronicle of the Turf, Field, Sports, and the Stage. Vol. 18, No. 20–Vol. 123, No. 15. July 1868–April 1892. Then, *Spirit of the Times and the New York Sportsman.* A Chronicle of Racing, Trotting, Field, Sports, Aquatics, Athletics, and the Stage. Vol. 123, No. 16–Vol. 144, No. 23. May 1892–3 December 1902. Weekly. [Absorbed by the *New York Sportsman,* 7 May 1892. With 6 September 1873 (Vol. 86, No. 4), new volume numbering was adopted by Wilkes.] CtY, DLC (1-7, [18]-28-144), MiD (12-13, 52-53, 58-60, 70-77, 79-103), MiDU ([14-144]), NN (1-[11]-[26-28]-29, [86-90]-144)

1860

39. *Daily Dramatic Review.* Cincinnati, Ohio. Vols. 1-2, No. 35. [?] 1860–9 February 1861. Daily (except Saturday and Sunday). [139 issues.] MiU (missing Vol. 1, Nos. 1-12)

1861

40. *The Programme.* New York, New York: Published by Charles McLachlan and Company. 1861–[after 1873]. Six days a week. [See Franklin William Scott, *Newspapers and Periodicals of Illinois, 1814-1879* (rev. and enlarged ed.; Springfield, Illinois, 1910). Scott says that the publisher was G. W. Morris from 1868 to 1870; P. H. Massic was editor and publisher in 1870 and publisher in 1871. In 1873 Marsh and Baker were publishers (p. 78).] NHi (Vol. 7, No. 1897–Vol. 7, No. 2051. 1 January 1863–6 July 1863).

1864

41. *Daily Dramatic News.* Cairo, Illinois: Published by H. L. Goodall, in the Interest of the Cairo Athenaeum. Winter 1864–1865. [Scott, p. 36.]

1865

42. *Daily Dramatic Chronicle.* San Francisco, California: [Wm. P. Harrison], Published at No. 417 Clay Street; Vol. 2 on, "Published by G. & C. De Young, and then by Chas. De Young & Co., No. 606 Montgomery Street. Vols. 1-8, No. 40. 31 January 1865–31 August 1868. Daily. Then, Vol. 8, No. 41. 1 September 1868 superseded by the *Daily Morning Chronicle.* Then, by *Dramatic Review* which merged 11 January 1869 with *Figaro* to form the *Figaro and Dramatic Review.* [This latter information is contained in a letter from the librarian at the University of California, Berkeley. This magazine was supposedly started by Charles De Young, when he was eighteen years old, and by his brother Mike, two years younger.] CU

43. *Stage.* Edited by D. H. Hopkinson. New York, New York. Vols. 1-32. 1865–1880. Irregular. [See Mott, III, 199.] CtY ([3, 10-14, 18, 30]), MWA ([1, 16, 19, 24]), NN ([2, 7-8, 10-11, 13, 15-16, 18, 31-32])

1866

44. *The Dramatic Mirror.* A Journal of Theatrical Literature Contributed by Members of the Dramatic Profession. Edited by T. C. Faulkner. New York, New York: Faulkner. Vol. 1, No. 1. October 1866. Monthly. MB

45. *Prompter.* Philadelphia, Pennsylvania. Vol. 1, Nos. 1-5. September 1866–January 1867. Monthly. MH (Nos. 1-3, [5])

46. *The Stage.* An Evening Theatrical Paper. Philadelphia, Pennsylvania:

John W. Forney, Jr., Publisher, S. W. Corner 7th and Chestnut Streets. Vol. 1, Nos. 1-54. 29 January–31 March 1866. Daily (six days a week). MH (missing Nos. 1, 40)

1867

47. *The Daily Critic.* San Francisco, California. [Published variously by] Charles De Lacy & Co., Thos. W. Reid & Co., and Wm. A. Calhoun. Vols. 1-2, No. 54. 23 September 1867–23 May 1868. Daily (except Sundays). [The 23 May issue may not be the final one.] C-S (incomplete), CU-B (incomplete)

48. *Opera House Programme.* Chicago, Illinois: G. S. Utter and Company. [1867?–1870?]. Daily. [Scott, p. 91.]

49. *Sporting Times and Theatrical News.* Boston, Massachusetts: John Stetson. Vols. 1-10. 1867[?]–1872. Weekly. MH (incomplete), MWA ([2]-[7]), NN ([6-7])

1868

50. *The Critic.* Washington City, D.C. Vol. 1, Nos. 1-114. 31 August 1868– 9 January 1869. Daily (except Sundays). DLC

51. *New England Base Ballist.* A Weekly Journal, An Advocate of the National Game, Field, Sports and the Drama. Boston, Massachusetts. Vol. 1, Nos. 1-22. 6 August–31 December 1868. Weekly. MB

52. *The Season.* New York, New York. Vol. 3, No. 415–Vol. 7, No. 1037. 20 October 1868–29 August 1870. Daily. [I have not been able to locate any issues before No. 415.] NN (missing all before Vol. 3, No. 415)

1869

53. *The Folio.* A Monthly Journal of Music, Drama, Art, and Literature. Boston, Massachusetts. Vols. 1-42, No. 10. September 1869–October 1895. Monthly. [The subtitle varies.] DLC (1-11, 20-[23-26]-[31-32, 35-37]), MB, MH (2-[31], 35), NN (18-36, [38]-[42])

54. *Ladies Theatrical Bouquet.* [Distributed free to ladies at some ten theaters.] New York, New York: 142 Fulton Street, 2nd floor. 27 November 1869; 26 March 1870. [These are the only two issues which I have been able to locate.] NN

1870

55. *L'Entr'Acte.* Journal des théâtres, litteraire et artistique. Edited by Alfred Mercier and L. E. Marchand. New Orleans, Louisiana: Publiée par Alfred Mercier et L. E. Marchand. Vol. 1, Nos. 1-2. 19–26 November 1870. Weekly. [A theater chronicle, to be published only during the

theater season. I have not been able to learn the final date of publication, as the Howard Memorial Library has only two issues.] LNHT

56. *Figaro*. San Francisco, California: J. P. Bogardus. Vols. 4-71 [with many irregularities]. 22 July 1870–17 December 1904. Daily (irregular). [I have not been able to find a location for any of the issues in the first three volumes.] NN (film; only a scattering of the total number of issues)

57. *The Season*. An Independent Critical Journal. New York, New York. Vols. 1-3, No. 25. 8 October 1870–23 September 1871. Weekly. [Vol. 2, No. 2–Vol. 3, No. 25 (14 January–23 September 1871), called a New Series. Various numbers have a supplement. The title varies slightly. Relates largely to music and drama in New York. United with *Our Society* to form *Our Society and the Season*.] MB (1-2), MH, NN (1-[3])

1871

58. *American Society*. Fashions, Society, Music, Education, Church, Masonic, Military, Theatre, Fine Arts, Clubs, Yachting, Turf and Other Pastime Intelligence. New York, New York: New York and Hartford Publishing Co., New York Times Building, No. 41 Park Row, Printing House Square. Vol. 1, Nos. 1-3. 13–27 May 1871. Weekly. [The publisher changes.] DLC

59. *The Boston Ray*. Edited by H. A. M'Glenen. Boston, Massachusetts: Published Every Afternoon by Lawrence & Page, 34 Water Street. Vols. 1-2. 2 September 1871–17 January 1873. Daily. DLC (missing Vol. 2), MBAt ([1-2])

1872

60. *American Athenæum*. Literature, the Fine Arts, Music and the Drama. New York, New York, and Boston, Massachusetts. Vol. 1, Nos. 1-8. 22 September–9 November 1872. New Series. Vol. 1, No. 1. 29 March 1873. DLC (missing since at least 1932), MWA (New Series, Vol. 1, No. 1)

61. *The Arcadian*. Edited by G. H. Butler (1875); L. Engel (to 1877); J. W. Tooley (1877-1878). New York, New York: 89 Nassau Street [later 128 Fulton Street]. Vols. 1-8, No. 2. 18 September 1872–12 January 1878. Weekly. [Publication suspended from 24 May to 6 September 1877.] DLC, MB (1-[4]), MH ([1-7]), MWA ([2-5, 7]), NN (1, 3-[4])

62. *Dexter Smith's Musical, Literary, Dramatic and Art Paper*. Edited by Dexter Smith. Boston, Massachusetts: Dexter Smith. Vols. 1-14, [Nos. 1-84]. January 1872–December 1878. Monthly. CtY, DLC(incomplete), MB, MH([1-2]-[6]-[8]-13-14), NN([3-5]-[8-11, 13])

1873

63. *Echo.* Music, Literature, Art, Drama. Edited by Albert A. Hill. Providence, Rhode Island: Cory Brothers, 120 Westminster Street. Vols. 1-2, No. 1. September 1873–September 1874. Monthly. DLC ([1]), RPB

64. *Musical Bouquet.* A Monthly Periodical Devoted to Music, Art, Literature, and Useful Information Connected with the Drama. New York, New York. Vol. 1, No. 1. October 1873. Monthly. DLC

1874

65. *New York Clipper Annual.* Containing Theatrical, Musical and Sporting Chronologies. New York, New York: The F. Queen Publishing Company. [Seven volumes.] 1874–1901. Annual. DLC, MB, MH

1875

66. *Brooklyn Daily Stage.* Established, 1874. Devoted to the Drama, Music, and Art. Brooklyn, New York. 20 September 1875–20 October 1879. Daily. [The issues are not numbered. Discusses plays at Brooklyn Theatre, Hooley's New Theatre, Olympic Theatre, New Park Theatre, and Academy of Music.] NN(very incomplete; some eighty-seven issues)

67. *Music Trade Review.* Edited by J. C. Freund. New York, New York. Vols. 1-10, No. 5. 3 November 1875–18 October 1879. Then, *Musical Times and Music Trade Review.* Vol. 10, No. 6–Vol. 11, No. 11. November 1879–10 January 1880. Semimonthly (3 November 1875–18 October 1878); weekly (2 November 1878–10 January 1880). CtY ([2]-10), LNHT (1, 3-11), NN

68. *New York Dramatic News.* Edited by C. A. Byrne. New York, New York. Vols. 1-65. 2 October 1875–May 1919. Irregular. [Title changes slightly. Vol. 53 repeated in numbering. See Mott, III, 198.] CoD (64-65), MB(12-13, [15]-16-21-[22]-23-[24]-25-26, [29]-[30], [33-34]), NN (1-4, [16-17, 27-29, 31-32], 34, [36], 38, 42, 45, 47, 55, 62-63)

1876

69. *New York Figaro.* New York, New York. Vol. 1, Nos. 1-11. 27 September–16 December 1876. Then, *The Illustrated Figaro.* Vol. 1, No. 12. 23 December 1876. Weekly. [I have not been able to locate the first three issues.] MH, NNHi

70. *New York Illustrated Times.* The Best Theatrical and Sporting Journal in America. New York, New York. Vols. 1-15. 14 October 1876–June 1884. Daily (irregular). [The subtitle varies. Supersedes *Day's Doings.*] DLC (1-[13]-15), NN (microfilm)

71. *Play-Bill.* (Chestnut Street Theatre). Philadelphia, Pennsylvania. Vols. 1-2, Nos. 1-40. 1 January 1876–21 May 1877. Weekly (irregular). [Three issues are dated 21 May 1877 and called Vol. 2, No. 40.] MH, NN, PHi ([1-2])

1877

72. *The Illustrated Dramatic & Sporting News.* Edited by Fred J. Engelhardt. New York, New York: 298 Broadway. Vol. 1, Nos. 1-13. 15 November 1877–18 January 1878. Then, *Frank Leslie Jr.'s Sporting and Dramatic Times.* Vol. 1, Nos. 14-23. 10 April 1878–5 June 1878. Weekly. [The place of publication changes to 35 East 17th Street.] NN

1878

73. *The Amusement World.* A Weekly Review of the Drama, Music, and the Fine Arts. Edited by Frank I. Jervis. Chicago, Illinois: William E. Smith, 69 Dearborn Street. Vol. 1, [No. 1?]. [4 December 1878?] New Series. Vol. 1, No. 2. 11 December 1878. Weekly. [The publication was never listed in the city directories.] ICHi

74. *Warrington's Musical Review, Music, Art, Drama, and Literature.* Edited by W. J. Warrington. New Orleans, Louisiana: W. J. Warrington. Vols. 1-7, No. 7. 1878[?]–August 1884. Monthly. LNHT (Vol. 7, No. 7)

1879

75. *The Illustrated Dramatic Weekly.* Devoted to the Interests of the Stage. Edited by Sydney Rosenfeld (25 January–25 June 1879); Champion Bissell (19 July–30 August 1879). New York, New York: Published at No. 120 Union Square. Vol. 1, Nos. 1-13. 25 January–7 May 1879. Then, *The Rambler and Dramatic Weekly.* Devoted to the Social World and the Interests of the Stage. New York, New York: Home Book Publishing Company. Vol. 1, No. 14–Vol. 2, No. 3. 14 May–30 August 1879. Weekly (irregular). [Twenty-nine issues. The subtitle changes.] DLC (incomplete), ICU (missing Vol. 1, Nos. 1-2, and Vol. 2, Nos. 1-3), ICU (incomplete), MB (missing Vol. 1, Nos. 1-4), MH ([1]-2), NjP ([1-2]), NN (missing Vol. 1, Nos. 1-2, 4, and Vol. 2)

76. *New York Figaro.* Belletristiche Wochenschrift für Theater, Musik, Kunst, Literatur und Unterhaltung. New York, New York. Vols. 1-3, No. 21. 9 September 1879–22 May 1881. New Series. Vols. 1-20. 17 September 1881–1900. [The subtitle varies slightly.] ICN (New Series, 13-20), NIC (1; New Series, Vol. 2, No. 41), NN (New Series, [2]-19).

77. *New York Mirror.* New York, New York. Vols. 1-95, Nos. 1-2249. [Vols. 84-85 incorrectly numbered Vols. 94-95.] 1879–19 January 1889. Then,

New York Dramatic Mirror. 26 January 1889–10 February 1917. Then, *Dramatic Mirror.* 17 February 1917–9 October 1920. Then, *Dramatic Mirror and Theatre World.* 16 October 1920–24 December 1921. Then, *New York Mirror* 31 December 1921–April 1922. Weekly (monthly, beginning in April 1922). [Vols. 85-93 omitted in numbering. A most important theatrical periodical. Edited by H. G. Fiske, 1879–22 November 1911. Absorbed *The Theatre World,* 16 October 1920. See Mott, III, 199.] IC (1-[81]-[84]-85), NN (1-[81]-[84]-85), WaS (64-[65-66]-[83]-95)

1880

78. *Dramatic Magazine.* Devoted to Dramatic Art and Literature. New York, New York: Published by Dramatic Magazine Co., 816 Broadway. Vol. 1, Nos. 1-7. May 1880–February 1881. Monthly (irregular). [Vol. 2.] Second Series. Conducted by Lisle Lester. New York, New York: 32 East 14th Street. Vol. 2, Nos. 1-7. August 1881–August 1882. Irregular. MH (missing Vol. 1, No. 6; Vol. 2, Nos. 2, 5-7), NN (missing Vol. 2, No. 2)

79. *Orchestra.* A Monthly Journal Devoted to Music and the Drama, Military and Brass Bands. Boston, Massachusetts. Nos. 1-5. January–May 1880 Monthly. DLC (missing Nos. 1, 3-4)

1881

80. *Byrne's Dramatic Times.* A Newspaper Published Weekly and Devoted to the Drama, Music, Society, and Art. Edited by C. A. Byrne. New York, New York: Published by C. A. Byrne, 860 Broadway. Vols. 1-9, No. 26. 1881–11 September 1886. Then, *Dramatic Times.* Vols. 10-23. 18 September 1886–19 August 1893. Weekly. [17 December 1887–1889, also called New Series. Vols. 3-4. Mott (IV, 260) says that it merged into the *New York Dramatic Times,* 1896.] C ([1-3, 8-9]), NN ([2-3]-[6-8]-9)

81. *The Critic.* A Fortnightly Review of Literature, the Fine Arts, Music and Drama. New York, New York. Vols. 1-3. 1881-1883. New Series. Vols. 1-49, No. 3. 1884–1906. Biweekly. [15 January 1881–September 1906. Vols. 4-32 (1884–1898), also as New Series. Vols. 1-29. Subtitle varies. January–June 1884 as *Critic and Good Literature;* 1905, *Critic and Literary World.* Merged into *Putnam's Monthly, and the Critic.*] C, CU, CtW, CtY, DLC, IU, IaU, MB, MH, MiU, NB, NIC, NN, NbU, NjP, OClW, PPi, PSC, RPB, WHi

82. *L'Opéra et ses Hôtes.* Sous la direction: G. de Beauplan. Album Illustré avec photographies et esquisses biographiques par F. Armant. Nouvelle Orléans, Louisiana: edité à l'Imprimerie du Croisant, 123 Rue de Chartres. Nos. 1-5. 1881. Irregular (during the season). [The purpose

was to give information about Beauplan's company, as well as to review the operas presented during the season of 1880/81.] LNHT, LNSM, MH

83. *The Stage.* Springfield, Massachusetts: L. H. Orr, Publisher, P. O. Box 1073. Vols. 1-11, No. 8. 29 September 1881–25 May 1882. [110 issues.] Irregular. [House Programme of the Opera House. Distributed at each performance. Vol. 4 has two issues numbered 10.] CtY (missing Vol. 2, Nos. 5, 10; Vol. 4, No. 3; Vol. 6, Nos. 2, 3, 5; Vol. 8, No. 7; Vol. 10, No. 2; Vol. 11, Nos, 2, 4, 6)

84. *The Theatrical Guide of the New England States.* Boston, Massachusetts: M. H. Johnson & Co. [Vols. 1-2.] 1880/81–1881/82. Annual. DLC

1882

85. *Music.* A Review. Edited by John C. Freund. New York, New York: 30 East 14th Street. Vols. 1-2, No. 3. 7 January–22 April 1882. Then, *Music and Drama.* A Review of the Stage, Art, Literature and Society. [Some variation in the title.] Vol. 2, No. 4–Vol. 5, No. 1. 29 April 1882–6 January 1883. Then, *Weekly Music and Drama.* Vol. 5, No. 2–Vol. 7, No. 20. 13 January–1 December 1883. Weekly. [Superseded by *Freund's Music and Drama.* Vol. 7, No. 13, omitted in the numbering.] MB (1-[7]), MH (missing Vol. 7), NN (incomplete)

86. *San Francisco Dramatic Brevities.* Drama, Music, Art. Edited by F. L. Fischer and R. D. Milne. San Francisco, California: Fischer & Walter. Vol. 1, No. 25. 6 May 1882. Weekly. [I have not been able to locate any other issues. Running title: *The Dramatic Brevities.*] NN (Vol. 1, No. 25)

87. *The Theatre.* A Weekly Journal of the Stage. New York, New York: Published by the Metropolitan Printing Office. Vol. 1, Nos. 1-19. 5 August–9 December 1882. Then, *The Theatre and Dramatic World.* Vol. 1, Nos. 20-21. 16–23 December 1882. Weekly. DLC (missing Nos. 13-21), MH (missing Nos. 11, 20-21), NN (missing Nos. 9-21), NNC

1883

88. *Freund's Music and Drama.* New York, New York. Vols. 1-17. 10 November 1883–23 January 1892. Weekly. [Supersedes *Music and Drama.* Vols. 1-3, No. 7, as *Freund's Weekly.*] CtY ([1]-[3-4]-[10-17]), MB (1-[2-8]-16), NN (1-[3-4]-17)

89. *The Keynote.* Music, Art, Drama, Literature. New York, New York: John J. King, 38 East 40th Street. Vols. 1-[19], No. 1. 24 November 1883–January 1897. Weekly (monthly). [The subtitle varies. Absorbed by *Music Trade Review*, 13 February 1897.] CL (1-11), NN (1-[6]-[12], 14-15, 17-19), WM (1-18)

90. *Musical Observer.* A Review of Music, Art and Drama. Boston, Massachusetts. Vols. 1-2, No. 17. 8 December 1883–12 April 1884. Weekly. DLC [1-2]

91. *Oriole Tidings.* Devoted to Art, Literature, Music, Drama, Society and Home Culture. A local Record of the Doings of the Day. Baltimore, Maryland: Published by H. J. Conway. Vols. 1-3, No. 30. 1 September 1883–20 March 1886. Weekly. [134 issues. Official Organ of the Academy of Music.] DLC

92. *Shakespeariana.* Philadelphia, Pennsylvania: Leonard Scott Publishing Co., 1104 Walnut Street. [Vols. 6-10 published in New York.] Vols. 1-6. November 1883–1889. Then, *Shakespeariana.* A Critical and Contemporary Review of Shakespearian Literature. Conducted by the Shakespeare Society of New York. Vols. 7-10. 1890–October 1893. Monthly (through Vol. 6); quarterly (beginning with Vol. 7. 1890). [Nos. 1-90 reprinted, AMS Press, catalogue, 1968.] CSt, CU, CaOTP, CtY, DFo, DLC, ICN, IU, InU, MH, MiU, MnU, NN, NNC, OU, PU

1884

93. *Charles M. Cashin's Amusement Guide with Theatre Diagrams.* For Week Ending April 26 [1884]. Boston, Massachusetts. April 1884. [I have not been able to discover any other issues.] MB

94. *Harry Miner's American Dramatic Directory for the Season of 1884-'85.* A Complete Directory of the Dramatic and Operatic Professions and a Guide to the Opera Houses, Theatres and Public Halls of America. Together with Much Other Information of Value to the Amusement Profession. Edited by Harry Miner. New York, New York: Wolf & Palmer Dramatic Publishing Company, 81 and 83 Elm Street. 1884/85–1887/88. CtY (1884/85), NN, NNC (1884/85, 1887/88)

1885

95. *Dramatic News.* A Journal Devoted to the Theatrical Profession. . . . Sacramento, California. 24 June 1885–12 June 1886. [Clarence Gohdes, *Literature and Theatre of the States and Regions of the U.S.A.* (Durham, North Carolina, 1967), p. 23.]

96. *New York Amusement Gazette.* Programme of Operas, Theatres, Concerts and Other Entertainments. Edited by F. T. Law. New York, New York: 949 Broadway. Vols. 1-19, No. 20. 5 September 1885–25 December 1893. Weekly. [429 issues. Vol. 15, Nos. 1-3, are numbered 11-13. See Mott, IV, 260. The subtitle varies.] DLC ([4]-[8]), MB (1-[13]-[16-18]), NN (1-[16]-19)

97. *Shakespeare Society of New York Papers.* [Later, *Publications.*] New

York, New York. Nos. 1-14. 1885–1926. Irregular. [No. 13 withdrawn by its author. Reprinted, AMS Press catalogue, 1968.] CtY, ICN (Nos. 1-12), NN (Nos. 1-12, 14)

1886

98. *The Opera Glass.* New York, New York: Ernest H. Adams, Publisher, 11 Pine Street. Vol. 1, Nos. 1-8. 16 January–6 March 1886. Weekly. [Consists chiefly of the programs of the leading New York theaters.] MH, NNHi

99. *The Theatre.* An Illustrated Weekly Magazine. Drama, Music, Art. Edited by Deshler Welch. New York, New York: Theatre Publishing Company. 31 and 33 West 23rd Street. Vols. 1-9, Nos. 1-192. 20 March 1886–27 April 1893. Weekly (with monthly or biweekly issues in the summer, Vols. 1-7; irregular). [Vol. 8 consists of five numbers (Nos. 179-183), issued January–Summer 1892. Vol. 9 consists of nine numbers (Nos. 184-192), issued February–April 1893. Vol. 6, Nos. 18-24, incorrectly listed on the cover as Vol. 6, Nos. 17-25.] DLC, ICN (missing Vol. 9), MH (1-[9]), MiU (Vols. 1-6), NN (Vols. 1–[8]), MWA

1888

100. *Dramatic Year.* Brief Criticisms of Important Theatrical Events in the United States, with a Sketch of the Season in London, by William Archer. Edited by Edward Fuller (1887-1888). Boston, Massachusetts: Tichnor & Co. 1888. [Annual?] DLC, MH, NN, PU

101. *The New York Mirror Annual.* And Directory of the Theatrical Profession for 1888. Edited by Harrison Grey Fiske. New York, New York: The New York *Mirror*, 145 Fifth Avenue. 1888. Annual. CtY, DLC, MH, MiU, NN

102. *The Playgoer's Year-Book for 1888.* Story of the Stage [for] the Past Year with Especial Reference to Boston. By Charles E. L. Wingate. Boston, Massachusetts: Stage Publishing Company. 1888. [Annual?] DLC, MB, NN

103. *Portrait Album.* Lights of Music and the Stage. New York, New York: McKinley and Wohltman. Vol. 1, No. 1. January 1888. Monthly. [Although the Library of Congress lists the magazine, with a call number, it is no longer present in the library.]

104. *The Stage.* Edited by Morton McMichael. Philadelphia, Pennsylvania: The Stage Publishing Co., Ltd., N. W. Corner Tenth and Chestnut Street. Nos. 1-67. 29 September 1888–4 January 1890. Weekly. CtY (1-52), MH, NN (missing Nos. 25, 28-67), PP (missing Nos. 54-67)

1889

105. *The Amusement Bulletin*. Contains the Theatrical, Society, Athletic, Musical, Literary and Personal News of the Week. Edited by H. C. Burdick. Vol. 1, No. 26–Vol. 3, No. 3. 29 March 1890–18 October 1890. New York, New York: Amusement Bulletin, 30 Union Square [through Vol. 1, No. 8, 23 November. Then, Published by The Travelers Publishing Co., 30 Union Square]. Vols. 1-3, No. 3. 5 October 1889–18 October 1890. Weekly. NN (missing Vol. 2, Nos. 1-2, 7-9)

106. *Le Chat Noir*. A Review of the Players. Edited by C. M. S. McLellan (to Vol. 2, No. 17); A. A. Reed (Vol. 2, Nos. 18-19). New York, New York: John O. Patten, Proprietor and Manager, 4 East 54th Street (22 February–12 July 1889), 1285 Broadway (19 July–27 December 1889). Vols. 1-2, No. 8. 22 February 1889–11 October 1889. Weekly. Then, *The Black Cat*. A Review of the Players. Vol. 2, Nos. 9-19. 18 October–27 December 1889. Weekly. MH, NN (incomplete)

107. *Musical Advance*. Devoted to Music, Art, Literature, Voice and Drama. Minneapolis, Minnesota. Vol. 1, Nos. 1-6. February–July 1889. Monthly. DLC (missing Nos. 3-5)

108. *New York Saturday Review*. Science, Art, Literature, Society, Politics, Music, Drama. New York, New York. Vols. 1-4. 5 October 1889–11 April 1891. Weekly. MH ([1-4])

109. *Poet Lore*. A Quarterly of World Literature. Boston, Massachusetts. Vols. 1-57, No. 2. 1889–Summer 1953. Quarterly. [Suspended publication December 1901–October 1902; 1931–1932. Vols. 1-25 indexed by Frank R. Holmes, 1916.] CLU, CU, CtY, ICN, ICU, IEN, IU, MB, MH, MiU, NIC, NN (missing Vol. 41), OCl

1890

110. *The Dramatic Mirror Quarterly*. Edited by Harrison Grey Fiske. New York, New York: The Dramatic Mirror. Vol. 1, Nos. 1-3. June 1890–January 1891. Quarterly. MB (No. 1), MH

111. *Philadelphia Music and Drama*. [Edited by C. Bloomingdale.] Philadelphia, Pennsylvania: Music and Drama Co. Vols. 1-3. 1890–1892. NN ([3])

112. *Stageland*. A Journal of Philadelphia Theatrical Information. Philadelphia, Pennsylvania. Vol. 1, Nos. 1-10. 1 September–3 November 1890. Weekly. [The subtitle varies.] MH (missing No. 5)

113. *20th Century Review*. Artists, Musicians, Men of Letters, the Drama. Buffalo, New York. Vol. 1, Nos. 1-4. January–April 1890. Monthly. MB, NBu, NN

1891

14. At *Home and Abroad*. A Monthly Review Devoted to Music and the Kindred Arts. Edited by Albert D. Hubbard. November 1891–June 1892. New York, New York: Albert D. Hubbard Publishing Co. Vols. 1-8, No. 4. November 1891–October 1895. Monthly. DLC (1-4, to June 1893), NN (4, 7-8), NcD ([6])

1893

15. *The Amusement Globe*. Devoted to the Dramatic, Theatrical, Musical, Vaudeville and Circus Professions. New York, New York: W. W. Randall, 1180 Broadway. [Nos. 8-23 published by the Amusement Globe Publishing Company, W. W. Randall, President.] Vol. 1, Nos. 1-23. 30 August 1893–31 January 1894. Weekly. NN

16. *Cleveland Amusement Gazette*. Cleveland, Ohio. Vols. 1-5. 30 September 1893–30 November 1895. Then, *The Critic and Amusement Gazette*. A Weekly Critical Review of the Stage, Music, Art, Literature, Society and Local Cycling. Edited by Charles W. Mears (Vol. 1, Nos. 1-2); William B. Thom. Cleveland, Ohio: Emil Grossman & Bro., Publishers and Proprietors. New Series. Vols. 1-3, No. 22. 7 December 1895–8 May 1897. [Seventy-two issues.] Weekly (during theater season). [4 Vols. in New Series.] OCl, NN (New Series, Vols. [3-4])

17. *Dramatic Chronicle*. Olympia, Washington. [Vol. 1, Nos. 1-9. 18 October 1893–23 April 1894?] Irregular. [My information comes from Yale University library.] CtY

18. *Dramatic Studies*. Edited by Alfred Allen (beginning with Vol. 2). New York, New York: Published by the American Academy of the Dramatic Arts. Berkeley Lyceum. 44th Street near 5th Avenue. Copyright 1893 by Franklin H. Sargent. Vols. 1-2, No. 9. October 1893–April 1899. Monthly (irregular). [Not published between 1894 and 1897.] MB (no title page for Vol. 1), NN ([1-2])

19. *Opera*. New York, New York. Vols. 1-2, Nos. 1-68. 1893–15 October 1895. Irregular. [I have not been able to locate any issues before No. 53.] MH (Nos. 53-68)

1894

20. *Billboard*. Weekly Theatrical Newspaper. Cincinnati, Ohio: Billboard Publishing Co., 2160 Patterson Street. Vols. 1-72. 1 November 1894–31 December 1960. Weekly (monthly, 1894–May 1900). [There are various errors in numbering. The title varies: 1894–March 1897, the title is *Billboard Advertising*. For the years 1921-1931 and 1939-1941 there is a fall issue which features annual news of the legitimate stage. For other years the annual news is issued separately. See *Billboard Index*

of the New York Legitimate Stage. Vols. 51-54, which cover the years 1939-1942, contain a September issue which includes a separately paged supplement. The magazine combined after 31 December 1960 with *Funspot* to form *Amusement Business.*] NN (Vols. 1-67, 1894–1955, are on film; 68-72), TN, WM

121. *Gallery of Players.* From the Illustrated American. Edited by Austin Brereton (No. 1); Charles F. Nirdlinger (No. 2); Maxwell Hall (Nos. 3-6); Henry Austin (Nos. 7-9); Arthur Hoeber (No. 11). New York, New York: The Illustrated American Publishing Company. Nos. 1-12. 1894–1897. Quarterly. [The title varies.] IU, MB (missing Nos. 10, 12), NN (incomplete)

122. *The Jury.* Edited by Clyde Laurence Parke (10 February 1894); Charles S. Hathaway (5 May 1894–23 June 1894). Detroit, Michigan: The Jury Company, No. 11, W. Atwater Street. Vols. 1-2, No. 8. 3 February–23 June 1894. Weekly. [Twenty issues.] MiD

123. *The New York Dramatic Chronicle.* Tyson's Official Programme. A Weekly Giving Full & Official Casts of All Plays of the Week and Other Dramatic Intelligence. Edited by Frank V. Strauss. New York, New York: Published by Frank V. Strauss, 108-114 Wooster Street. Vols. 1-4, No. 26. 3 September 1894–24 August 1896. Weekly. [104 issues.] NN

124. *Opera.* Chicago, Illinois. Vols. 1-2. 1894–1895. Weekly (Vol. 1); biweekly (Vol. 2). MH ([1-2])

125. *The Opera Glass.* A Musical and Dramatic Magazine. Boston, Massachusetts: Opera Glass Publishing Company, 15 School Street. Vols. 1-5, No. 12. 17 February 1894–December 1898. Monthly. [On cover of Vol. 1, No. 1, "The Opera Glass. Glimpses of Musical and Dramatic Life." Fifty-nine issues. For the Boston Theatre.] ICN (missing Vol. 1, No. 1), ICU, MB, MH, NN, PP

126. *Shakespeare.* The Journal of the Edwin Booth Shakespeare League. Philadelphia, Pennsylvania. Vol. 1. May 1894–May 1895. Monthly. [No number issued for July 1894.] DLC, IC, NN

127. *Shakespeariana Club.* Grand Rapids, Michigan. 1894/95. Annual. [Although the New York Public Library did have a copy at one time, it no longer possesses the work. I have been unable to locate a copy in any other library.]

1895

128. *American Shakespeare Magazine.* Edited by Anna Randall-Diehl. New York, New York: Shakespeare Magazine Company. Vols. 1-4, No. 3. January 1895–March 1898. Biweekly and monthly. [Vol. 1 has the title, *The Fortnightly Shakespeare.* Reprinted AMS Press catalogue, 1968.] DLC ([1, 3-4]), MB ([1-2]-4), MH ([2-3]), MiU

9. *Footlights.* A Weekly Journal for the Theatre-Goer. Philadelphia, Pennsylvania. Vols. 1-4, No. 10. 1895–14 November 1896. Weekly. [I have been unable to locate any information on the date of the first issue.] MB ([1]), MH ([4])

0. *The Looker-On.* Musical, Dramatic, Literary. Edited by W. H. Fleming. New York, New York: Published by Whittingham & Atherton, 8 Broad Street. Vols. 1-4, No. 6. [Twenty-one issues.] October 1895–June 1897. Monthly. [The place of publication changes.] ArU, CL, DLC, ICN (wanting May–June 1897), ICU, NN, NPV, WHi

1. *Mahatma.* The Only Paper in the United States Devoted to the Interests of Magicians, Spiritualists, Mesmerists, etc. Edited by George H. Little (to January 1900); Walter G. Peterkin (to August 1901); Francis Fritz (September 1901–February 1906). New York, New York: 493 6th Avenue. Vol 1, Nos. 1-12. March–June 1895. Then, *The Vaudeville*, Devoted to Theatricals. "Late Mahatma." Lawrence & Little, Editors and Proprietors. Vols. 2-9, No. 8. [Whole No. 118.] July 1898–February 1906. Weekly, monthly (irregular). [The publication history, and title changes are somewhat tangled. For what volumes make up the magazine, see articles in *Sphinx*, and in *Magicol*, II (February 1952), 4-5.] MH ([1]-[3]-9), NN (Vol. 2, Nos. 1-12. July 1898–June 1899)

2. *The Stage.* (Hyperion Theatre. G. B. Bunnell Lessee and Manager). New Haven, Connecticut: The Price Lee & Adkins Co., Publishers, 206-10 Meadow Street. Nos. 1-166. 23 August 1895–3 June 1896. Irregular. CtY (incomplete)

3. *Vaudeville.* Devoted to Theatricals. New York, New York. Vol. 1, Nos. 9-10. November–December 1895. [I have not been able to locate any other issues.] NN (Vol. 1, Nos. 9-10)

1896

4. *The Cahn-Leighton Official Theatrical Guide.* (Successor to the Julius Cahn Official Theatrical Guide) Containing Authentic Information Regarding All Cities, Towns and Villages, Wherein Theatrical Organizations May Find a Theatre, Opera House or Hall to Exhibit in As Well As the Information Pretaining [sic] to These Places of Amusement, the Railroads, Express Companies, Newspapers, Bill Posters, Transfer Companies, Hotels, etc., Throughout the United States and Canada. New York, New York. 1896-1921. Monthly (irregular). [In 1921 it united with *Gus Hill Theatrical Guide and Moving Picture Directory.* The subtitle varies.] DLC (incomplete), NN (very incomplete)

5. *Lyceum Night and Declamation Day.* In the Interest of Literary, Dramatic & Social Entertainment. Philadelphia, Pennsylvania. Nos. 1-55. May 1896–March 1905. Monthly (except July and August. May 1896–January 1903); quarterly (from March 1903). [No numbers issued

January–February 1897; May 1897–December 1898; April–May 1902.] DLC

136. *The Torch.* Memphis, Tennessee: The Torch Publishing Company. Vol. 1, No. 1. October 1896. MB

1897

137. *The Critic.* A Journal of Amusements. Minneapolis, Minnesota. Vol. 1. 4 September 1897–21 May 1898. [Gohdes, p. 112.]

138. *Dramatic Magazine.* Chicago, Illinois: Dramatic Magazine Press, 356 Dearborn Street. Vols. 1-12. August 1897–January 1903. Monthly (with quarterly cumulative editions). [Not published April–July 1900.] DLC (missing all after Vol. 10, No. 3), NBuG, NN (missing all after Vol. 10, No. 3)

1898

139. *The Amusement Record.* Devoted to the Interests of Theatre-goers. Published Weekly in the Interests of Theatre-goers. New York, New York: The Amusement Record, 41 Union Square. George W. Roebling, Publisher. Vol. 2, Nos. 9-32. 14 November 1898–24 April 1899. Weekly. [The 24 April issue says that it is the last for the season, but hopes to publish again next season. I have not been able to locate any issues before Vol. 2, No. 9.] NN (missing all before Vol. 2, No. 9, and Nos. 10, 12, 18, and 27)

140. *Broadway Magazine.* New York, New York: Broadway Publishing Company, 1270 Broadway. Vol. 2, No. 7–Vol. 19, No. 3. October 1898–December 1907. Monthly. Then, *The New Broadway Magazine.* Vol. 19, No. 4–Vol. 20, No. 3. January 1908–December 1908. Then, *Hampton's Broadway Magazine.* Vol. 21, No. 4–Vol. 27, No. 3. October 1908–September 1911. Then, *Hampton's Columbian Magazine.* Vol. 27, No. 4–Vol. 27, No. 6. October 1911–January 1912. DLC, MB (1-7), MiD, NN (missing all before Vol. 2, No. 7), US ([1-23, 27-28])

1899

141. *Actors Society Monthly Bulletin.* Edited by Geo. F. Macintyre (Vol. 7, Nos. 5-7. May–July 1904); Georgia Earle (Vol. 7, Nos. 8-12. August 1904–July 1905); Theodore Fkiebus (Vol. 8, Nos. 8-9. August–September 1905); J. H. Greene (Vol. 8, No. 10. October 1905); W. D. Stone (Vol. 8, No. 11–Vol. 9, No. 7. November 1905–July 1906); Mark Ellsworth (Vol. 9, No. 8–Vol. 11, No. 2. August 1906–February 1908); Stokes Sullivan (Vol. 11, Nos. 3-5. March–May 1908). New York, New York: Actors Society of America, 131 West 40th Street. Vols. 1-11, No.

5. 1 March 1899–May 1908. Monthly. [Vol. 1 repeats No. 7 in the numbering.] NN ([1-4]-[11]), MiU (1-2), ViU ([7-9])

2. *The Cast.* Published Weekly for the Theatre and Amusement-Going Public of New York. New York, New York: H. P. Hanford, Editor and Publisher. Vols. 1-212, No. 2512. [The numbering is consecutive.] 1899–28 August 1954. Weekly. [Indexes bound in the first volume of each season. The *Bulletin of Bibliography* says that publication was suspended with Vol. 212, No. 2512.] ICN (missing all before No. 38); NN ([1-100]-212), N (1-5, 7-12, 14-[20]-26, [32]-[51]-[53-54]-[56])

3. *The Dramatic Review.* Boston, Massachusetts. Nos. 3-47. 23 September 1899 [*Boston Dramatic Review*]–28 July 1900. Weekly. [Much information is missing on this magazine.] DLC (missing Nos. 1-2, 4, 6-12, 15-19, 21-22, 24, 26-30, 32-41, 45-46), MB ([6-7]), MH ([6-7])

4. *Elite.* Journal of Society, Music and Drama. New Orleans, Louisiana: Published by Elite Publishing Co. Vols. 1-4, No. 1. December 1899–January 1902. Biweekly. LN, LNHT, LNSM

5. *The Impressionist.* Edited by Norma L. Munro. New York, New York: Norma L. Munro. Vol. 1, Nos. 1-12. November 1899–October 1900. Monthly. [See Mott, IV, 261.] DLC

6. *The Opera Glass.* Brooklyn, New York: 428 Park Row Building. Vols. 1-2, No. 26. 25 September 1899–24 December 1900. Weekly (during the season). [Fifty-two issues. Playbills. Later subtitle: Official Amusement Guide and Universal Program of Brooklyn Theatres.] NN

7. *The Roaster!* Offiziells Organ für den Jahrmarkt des Buffalo Turnverein. Buffalo, New York: National Hall, 385 & 387 Ellicott Strasse. Nos. 1-13. January–12 April 1899. Very irregular (with Nos. 7-12, issued daily). NN

8. *San Francisco Dramatic Review and Music and Drama.* Edited first by W. D. Wasson, and later by Chas. H. Farrell. [Chas. H. Farrell was Business Manager as early as 1900.] San Francisco, California: Dramatic Review Pub. Co., 22½ Geary Street; also, San Francisco Dramatic Review, 1095 Market Street, Room 207. Vols. 1-30. 9 September 1899–18 July 1914. Weekly. [The title of the magazine changed to *San Francisco Dramatic Review, Music and Drama*. The date of the change is uncertain, but the first copy of this title that the California State Library at Sacramento has is 4 January 1908. Their holdings consist of broken files, so that dating is a little uneven.] C (Vols. 1-2, 4 [two issues], 17-24, 28-29, 29-30 [lacks April 11])

1900

9. *Magician.* A Magazine of Magic. Springfield, Illinois. Nos. 1-7. 1900–January 1901. New Series. Vol. 1, Nos. 1-3. December 1901–September 1902. Irregular. NN (missing Nos. 2 and 3 of the original series)

150. *Our Players Gallery.* Edited by W. J. Thorold (1900–February 1901); Arthur Hornblower (May 1901–February 1927); Arthur Hornblower, and Arthur Hornblower, Jr. (November 1922–April 1923); Perriton Maxwell (March 1927–August 1929); Steward Beach (September 1929–April 1931). New York, New York: 26 West 33rd Street. Vol. 1, [Nos. 1-2]. 1900. Then, *The Theatre.* Vol. 1, No. 3–Vol. 26, No. 197. December 1900–July 1917. Then, *The Theatre Magazine.* Vols. 27–53, No. 4. August 1917–April 1931. Quarterly (October 1900–January 1901); monthly (May 1901–April 1931). [Vol. 1, Nos. 1-2, lack numbering. Vol. 39 repeated in numbering. Vol. 41 called Vol. 40. Nos. 1-361.] CLU, CtW, DLC, IC, ICN, ICU, IEN, IU, IaU, MB (1-52), MnS, MiU, MoU, NN, NhD, OCl, PPi, WM

151. *The San Francisco Theatrical Guide.* A Weekly Journal Adopted to the Theatrical Managers of San Francisco as Their Official Guide. Edited by Al. Dodge. San Francisco, California: 927 Market Street. Vol. 1, No. 4–Vol. 3, No. 15. 3 December 1900–17 February 1902. [I have been unable to locate the three initial issues.] C (3 December 1900–12 August 1901), NN (17 February 1902)

152. *Types.* Edited by Otis Fenner Wood. New York, New York: Published by Types Publishing Company, 70 Fifth Avenue. No. 10. 21 February 1900. [I have not been able to locate any other issues.] NN (No. 10)

1901 (See also *Theater Zshurnal*, Addenda, p. 86.)

153. *Buffalo Amusement Guide.* Buffalo, New York: 410 Ellicott Square. Vol. 1, No. 1. 30 March 1901. Weekly. [*Bulletin of Bibliography*, II (July 1901), 125.]

154. *Music and Stage.* New York, New York: 1123 Broadway. Vol. 1, Nos. 1-2. 1 December 1901–1 May 1902. Quarterly (irregular). [Published also in London and Paris.] DLC (missing No. 1), MH

155. *New Shakespeareana.* A Critical Contemporary Current Review of Shakespearean and Elizabethan Studies, Conducted by the Shakespeare Society of New York. New York, New York, and Westfield, New Jersey 1902–1909); Somerville, New Jersey: Unionist-Gazette Association 1910–1911). Vols. 1-10, No. 4 September 1901–December 1911. Quarterly. [Reprinted, AMS Press catalogue, 1968.] DLC, ICN, ICU, KU, MB, MH, MiU, MnU, MoK, MoS, NN, NNC, NjP, NJR, OU, PEa, WaS

156. *Theatre and Amusement Guide to Pittsburgh, Allegheny and Suburbs.* Allegheny, Pennsylvania. Vol. 1, No. 1. 28 October 1901. Weekly. DLC

157. *The Theatre Resumé.* Minneapolis, Minnesota: 630 Guaranty Building. Vol. 1, No. 1. December 1901. Monthly. [To be on the theater in Minneapolis for the preceding month.] MH

158. *"Tricks."* New York, New York: Published by "Tricks" Publishing Com-

pany, 496 Sixth Avenue. Vols. 1-2, No. 8. 1 June 1901–January 1903. [Eighteen issues.] MH ([1]-2), NN

1902 (See also *Echo*, Addenda, p. 86.)

59. *Footlights.* New York, New York. Vol. 1, No. 1. November 1902. Monthly. [*Bulletin of Bibliography*, III (April 1903), 79. Supposed to be the successor to *Play and Players*.]

30. *The Green Room.* Boston, Massachusetts: 610 Barrister's Hall. Vol. 1, No. 1. November 1902. Monthly. [*Bulletin of Bibliography*, III (January 1903), 60.]

31. *Johnny on the Spot.* Short Stories, Very Short Verse, Extremely Short Essays, Stage Doings, Terse, Twinkling, Tattle, and No Obituaries: A Weekly Periodical Devoted to Light Literature and Everything That Claims Devotion. Edited by H. R. R. Hertzberg. New Orleans, Louisiana: Published by H. R. R. Hertzberg, Proprietor. Vol. 1, Nos. 1-5. 1 February–1 March 1902. Weekly. LNHT (Vol. 1, No. 4)

32. *The Sphinx.* A Monthly Illustrated Magazine Devoted Exclusively to Magic and Magicians. Chicago, Illinois [later, New York, New York: 130 West 42nd Street]. Vols. 1-48, No. 12. March 1902–February 1950. Monthly. [The subtitle varies.] DLC (1-15, 30+), FU ([4]+), MH (1-[20]-24, 28-31, [34-39]), NN, PP (44, 46-48+)

33. *Theatre Journal and Family Friend.* New York, New York. Vols. 1-2, No. 11. 1902–15 February 1903. Irregular. WHi (missing Vol. 1)

34. *Theatrical Brokerage News.* New York, New York: The New York Theatrical Stock Exchange, 1440 Broadway. Vol. 1, Nos. 1-2. 1902. [No month is given on the two issues.] NN

1903

35. *Broadway Weekly.* Edited by R. B. Hennessy. New York, New York: Broadway Weekly Co., 121 W. 42nd Street. Vol. 1, No. 1. 18 February 1903. Weekly. [I have located no other issues.] DLC

36. *Bulletin of the National Art Theatre Society of New York.* New York, New York: 1440 Broadway. Nos. 1-8. [?] 1903–February 1904. Then, *The Drama.* Official Organ of the National Art Theatre Society. Edited by F. P. Delgado. Nos. 9-13. March 1904–January 1905. Monthly (irregular). [No. 2 is August 1903.] NN (missing Nos. 1, 3, 4)

37. *The Burr McIntosh Monthly.* Edited by Burr McIntosh (April 1903–March 1905); Clark Hobart (June 1906–December 1909). New York, New York: Burr McIntosh Publishing Co. Vols. 1-22, No. 86. April 1903–May 1910. Monthly. [No title pages or indexes were issued. Contains numerous theatrical portraits and pictures.] DLC, MB, MiD, NB, NN, PP (1-[21]-22), WaU ([1-21])

168. *Drama* (National Art Theatre Society). New York, New York. No. 1. 1903. Then, *National Art Theatre Society Bulletin*. Nos. 2-13. 1903–1905. MH (Nos. 6, 8), NN (Nos. 2, 5-13)

169. *The First Nighter*. New York, New York: 241 West 23rd Street. Vol. 1, No. 1. 25 November 1903. Weekly. [*Bulletin of Bibliography*, III (April 1904), 146.]

170. *Hebrew Actors Protective Union of New York Journal*. Herausgegeben vun die judische Aktoren Union zu seiner 4 ten Jahresfest. New York, New York: Lipschitz. 27 December 1903. NN

171. *New Alcazar Messenger*. Edited by James Crawford. San Francisco, California: Published by Belasco & Mayer. Vol. 1, No. 39–Vol. 2, No. 19. 24 August 1903–26 April 1909. Weekly (irregular). [Vol. 1, No. 51, is 7 December 1903, and Vol. 2, No. 3, is 3 February 1909.] Free. NN (Vol. 1, Nos. 39-42, 50-51; Vol. 2, Nos. 3, 10-16, 18-19)

172. *New York Inquirer*. A Smart Paper for Smart Persons. By Leander Richardson and Others. New York, New York: 109 West 42nd Street. Vols. 1-4, No. 11. 26 September 1903–3 September 1904. Weekly. [Nineteen issues. Primarily on the theater and stage.] MH ([2-4]), NN ([1-2]), NjP (1-10)

173. *Philadelphia Theatrical Guide*. Philadelphia's Official Weekly Amusement Guide. Philadelphia, Pennsylvania: Theatrical Guide Company, Publishers, 1214 to 1220 Filbert Street. Vol. 1, Nos. 1-10. 7 December 1903–8 February 1904. Weekly. [Contains the official programs of all the leading theaters in Philadelphia.] DLC (incomplete)

174. *The Stage Aspirant*. A Monthly Magazine Devoted to Dramatic Art. Edited by John William Schmidt. New York, New York: Published by the Stage Aspirant Publishing Company, 500 Fifth Avenue. Vol. 1, No. 1. November 1903. Monthly. NN

1904

175. *Die Dramatische Welt*. A monatliche Schrift vum Literatur, Kritik un dramatische Neues, speciell gewidmet dem judischen Theater. Redakirt von Jacob Gordin. [Judeo-German.] New York, New York. [Nos. 1-4.] 15 July–16 October 1904. Monthly. [English title, *The Dramatic World*.] NN

176. *The Iconoclast*. The Man Who Pays. A Publication with the Truth-Habit. Boston, Massachusetts: Issued by the Iconoclast Publishing Co., 6 Beacon Street. Vols. 1-7, No. 3. 3 December 1904–16 June 1906. Weekly. [Relates to actors on the American stage, and in Boston particularly.] MB ([3, 5-6]), MH ([1]-[3-7])

177. *New York Playhouses*. New York, New York: Meert and Easter Publishers, 1181 Broadway. 5 September 1904–11 February 1905. Weekly.

[The magazine was not published between 31 December 1904 and 4 February 1905.] NN (missing 3 and 31 December 1904)

78. *Stage.* Edited by Roland Burke Hennessey. New York, New York: 1269 Broadway. Vols. 1-4, No. 8. 24 September 1904–24 February 1906. Weekly. [See Mott, IV, 261.] DLC (missing Vol. 4), MH ([2-3]), NN ([2-3])

1905 (See also *Theater Zinger,* Addenda, p. 86.)

79. *Gotham Life Guide.* The Official Metropolitan Guide. New York, New York: 220 W. 42nd Street. 1905. Weekly. [*The Standard Periodical Directory,* 1967, New York, New York: Oxbridge Publishing Co., Inc., 1967, p. 306.]

80. *Once a Month.* New York, New York: Published by Alice Kauser, 1432 Broadway. Vol. 1, No. 1. October 1905. Monthly. NN

81. *The Play.* New York, New York: 1947 Broadway. Vol. 1, No. 1. October 1905. Monthly. [*Bulletin of Bibliography,* IV (April 1906), 107.]

82. *The Repertoire Magazine.* Brooklyn, New York: 1008 Fulton Street. Vol. 1, No. 1. December 1905. Monthly. [*Bulletin of Bibliography,* IV (April 1906), 108.]

83. *The Show.* A Magazine of Stage Cleverness. New York, New York: Published Monthly by Channing Pollock, Lyric Theatre Building. Vols. 1-3, No. 10. 1905–February 1908. Monthly. MH ([1-2]-3), NN (1-[2]-3)

84. *Variety.* New York, New York. Vols. 1–. 1905–. Weekly. [The subtitle varies. Editors change as do places of publication. The basic trade paper.] NN

1906

85. *The Amateur Thespian.* Brooklyn, New York: 227 Lincoln Road. Vol. 1, No. 1. January 1906. Monthly. [*Bulletin of Bibliography,* IV (April 1906), 122.]

86. *American International Musical and Theatrical Union, Inc., New York Bulletin.* New York, New York. Vols. 1-6, No. 1. September 1906–August 1912. Irregular. MdBJ (1-[2-6])

87. *Conjurer's Monthly Magazine.* Edited by Harry Houdini. New York, New York: Published by The Conjurer's Magazine Publishing Co., 278 West 113th Street. Vols. 1-2, No. 12. September 1906–August 1908. Monthly. DLC, ICN, MH, NN

88. *The Footlights.* Published Weekly for the Theatre and Amusement-Going Public of Washington, D.C. Official and Up-To-Date. Edited by Arthur B. Benson. Washington, D.C.: The Footlight Publishing Co., 628 Lou-

isiana Ave., N.W. Vol. 1, Nos. 1-13. 17 September–10 December 1906. Weekly. DLC

189. *The Green Room Book.* Or, Who's Who on the Stage. An Annual Bio-graphical Record of the Dramatic, Musical and Variety World. Edited by B. Hunt (1906–1909); J. Parker (in 1909). New York, New York. [Vols. 1-4.] 1906–1909. Annual. MB, NN (missing Vol. 3)

190. *The Modern Theatre.* New York, New York. Vol. 1, Nos. 1-6. November 1906–April 1907. Monthly. NIC, NN

191. *On Dit.* Devoted to All Things Pertaining to Society, an Exponent of the Drama, and an Advocate of All Measures That Would Tend to Advance the Welfare of the South and the Betterment of Mankind. Edited by Mrs. F. Maud Saks. New Orleans, Louisiana: Published by Mrs. F. Maud Saks. Vol. 1, Nos. 1-3. March–May 1906. Monthly. LNHT

192. *The Shakespeare Monthly and Literary Companion.* Edited by John Phin. New York, New York: 16 Thomas Street. Vol. 1, Nos. 1-2. March–April 1906. Monthly. CtY, MH, MiU

193. *The St. Louis Dramatic News.* Devoted to Theatrical Interests, Music and Conservatories, and Schools of Dramatic Art. Edited by Richard Spamer. St. Louis, Missouri: The Dramatic News Co., 322 Commercial Bldg. Vols. 1-6, No. 20. 5 December 1906–13 October 1909. Weekly. DLC, MoS.

194. *The Theatrical Star.* New York, New York: 19 Park Place. Vol. 1, No. 1. January 1906. Weekly. [*Bulletin of Bibliography*, IV (April 1906), 108.]

195. *The Touchstone.* Chicago, Illinois: Opera House Building. Nos. 1–5. January–May 1906. Monthly. DLC, MWA

196. *Vaudeville.* New York, New York: 1402 Broadway. Vol. 1, No. 1. August 1906. Bimonthly. [*Bulletin of Bibliography*, IV (January 1907), 159.]

1907

197. *The Art World.* Variously Amerikanische Ausgabe von *Bühne und Welt* or American edition of *Bühne und Welt*. Edited by H. S. Friedenthal (April–June 1907); V. Neuhaus (July 1907–July 1908). Denver, Colorado: Art World Publishing Co., 210 Appel Building. Vols. 1–2, No. 11. April 1907–July 1908. Monthly. [Bound into the Library of Congress set, between November and December 1907 issues are eight special issues, each of which bears the title, *The Art World: American Edition of "Bühne und Welt."* The issues are undated, but inside the front cover of each is a reference to a 1907 issue of the German edition of *Bühne und Welt*. An examination of the *Bühne und Welt* set indicates that the special issues in the *Art World* are identical with the regular issues in the German edition, even as to pagination. Following the

special issues are two others, each of which is undated, and has no cover title. The running title on the inside page is *The Art World: Deutsche Theatre Zeitung.* References to the theater performances would seem to indicate dates of October and November 1907.] DLC

198. *The Crest Magician.* An Illustrated Monthly Magazine Devoted to the Advancement of Magic and Magicians. New York, New York: 144 West 37th Street. Vol. 1, Nos. 1-5. November 1907–March 1908. Monthly. [United with *Crest Musical Bulletin* to form *Entertaining.*] DLC, NN

199. *Crest Musical Bulletin.* Devoted to Up-to-date Music and Musicians. New York, New York. Vol. 1, Nos. 1-7. October 1907–April 1908. Monthly. [United with *Crest Magician* to form *Entertaining.*] DLC

200. *The Opera House Guide.* Cincinnati, Ohio: 416 Elm Street. Vol. 1, No. 1. July 1907. Monthly. [*Bulletin of Bibliography,* V (January 1909), 155.]

201. *The Scandalizer.* Published in the Interests of the Members of the New York Hippodrome. New York, New York. Vol. 1, Nos. 1–8. 5 January–May 1907. Biweekly (monthly). NN (missing Vol. 1, No. 4)

202. *The Show World.* The Twentieth Century Amusement Weekly, Devoted Exclusively to the Profession of Entertainment. Chicago, Illinois: Show World Publishing Company. Vols. 1-8, No. 6. 29 June 1907–August 1911. Weekly. DLC ([1]), IC (1-[3]), NN ([1]-[6-7]-8)

203. *Theatre.* A Weekly Magazine. Salt Lake City, Utah: [Tribune Reporter Printing Co.]. Vols. 1-6, No. 13. 2 September 1907–25 November 1912. Weekly (irregular). MH

204. *Theatregoers Magazine.* New York, New York: Publications of the Theatregoers Club of America. Vol. 1, No. 1. March 1907. [Theatregoers Club of America Constitution, pp. 11-14.] MH

205. *Theatrical News.* Chicago, Illinois: Opera House Block. Vol. 1, No. 1. December 1907. Weekly. [*Bulletin of Bibliography,* V (April 1908), 87.]

1908

206. *Amusement World.* Chicago, Illinois: 164 E. Randolph Street. Vol. 1, No. 1. 18 January 1908. Weekly. [*Bulletin of Bibliography,* V (July 1908), 110.]

207. *Memphis Weekly Amusement Guide.* Memphis, Tennessee. Vol. 1, No. 1. July 1908. Weekly. [*Bulletin of Bibliography,* V (April 1909), 177.]

208. *New York Star.* New York, New York. Vols. 1-36, No. 4. 1908–2 April 1926. Weekly. [Absorbed by *Vaudeville News,* 16 April 1926, to form *Vaudeville News and New York Star.*] MH ([1-2, 22]), NN ([1, 13-19]-[30]-[34]-36)

209. *Theater Welt.* New York, New York. Vol. 1, Nos. 1-4. November 1908–February 1909. Monthly. [In Hebrew. English title: *Theatre World.*] NN

1909

210. *The Better Magazine.* A Magazine for Magicians. Bradford, Pennsylvania. 1909. [I have not been able to locate any issues other than those listed below.] MH (Vol. 5, 1909), NN (Vol. 5, 1909)

211. *The Boy Magician.* The Boy's Own Journal of Magic. Official Organ of the National Conjurers' Association. Edited by Charles J. Hagen (Vol. 1, No. 7–Vol. 3, No. 8. October 1909–February 1912); Francis C. Hill (Vol. 4, Nos. 1-7. March–September 1912). New York, New York: Presto Publishing Co., 433 East 76th Street. Vols. 1-2, No. 1. April 1909–March 1910. Then, *The American Magician.* Vol. 2, No. 2–Vol. 4, No. 7. April 1910–September 1912. Monthly (with some irregularities). [The subtitle varies.] MH (1-[3-4]), NN

212. *The Chorus.* A Paper for the Chorus and Small Part People of Our American Theatres. Edited by William H. Clifford. New York, New York: Chorus Publishing Company, Knickerbocker Building, 39th Street and Broadway. Vol. 1, Nos. 1-4. 6 February–May 1909. Weekly (Nos. 1-2); monthly (Nos. 3-4). NN

213. *The Dramatist.* A Journal of Dramatic Technology. Edited by Luther B. Anthony (1909-1923). Easton, Pennsylvania: The Dramatist Co. Vols. 1-23, No. 1. October 1909–January 1932. Quarterly. [The subtitle varies. Index of Vols. 1-20 (1909–1929) in Vol. 21.] ICU, IaU, InU, MH, MiU MnU, NN (to Vol. 20, No. 1), OU, PU

214. *Edward's Monthly.* Devoted to Magic, Magicians and Mystics. Buffalo, New York. Vols. 1-2, No. 3. 3 February 1909–May 1910. Monthly. [Merged into *Sphinx.*] MH, NN (1-[2])

215. *The Green Book Album.* A Magazine of the Passing Show. Chicago, Illinois: The Story-Press Corporation, Publishers, 158-164 State Street, Vols. 1-8, No. 1. January 1909–July 1912. Then, *The Green Book Magazine.* Vol. 8, No. 2–Vol. 26, No. 1. August 1912–July 1921. Monthly. [Vol. 8, Nos. 2-6, August–December 1912, incorrectly numbered as Vol. 13, Nos. 2-6.] CtY (incomplete), DLC (missing Vol. 10), MiU, NN (to Vol. 24)

216. *Idishe Bihne.* [*Jewish Stage.*] New York, New York. Vol. 1, Nos. 1-24. 19 November 1909–29 April 1910. Weekly. DLC, NN

217. *The Jewish Dramatic World.* New York, New York: 203 East Broadway. Vol. 1, No. 1. March 1909. Monthly. [*Bulletin of Bibliography*, V (July 1909), 207.]

218. *Musical Messenger.* A Newspaper Published in the Interest of the Opera

and Concert. New York, New York. Vol. 1, Nos. 1-2. 24 November–December 1909. Irregular. DLC

19. *The Opera News*. Devoted to Current and Future Musical Events and Appearing Intermittently During the Season. Philadelphia and New York: John Wanamaker, City Hall. Vols. 1-11, No. 1. 11 November 1909–10 January 1920[?]. Irregular (depending on the frequency of concerts). [Superseded by *Music Record and Opera News*, March 1921. There are frequent errors in the numbering.] CL (1-9), DLC (1-[3]-[8, 11]), IU (1, [10]), NN ([1]-[10-11])

20. *The Player*. Official Organ of the White Rats of America, Inc. Edited by Walter K. Hill. New York, New York: Published by the White Rats of America Publishing Company, 1553 Broadway. Vols. 1-9, No. 17. 10 December 1909–13 April 1917. Weekly. [The subtitle varies. Vol. 7 omitted in the numbering. Suspended between 21 November 1913 and 22 December 1916. Vol. 9, Nos. 1-17, called second series. By the Associated Actors and Artistes of America under its earlier names, White Rats of America and White Rat Actors Union of America (10 December 1909–2 December 1910) with the Associated Actresses of America.] DLC (5-8), IU (5-8), NN (incomplete)

21. *Stageland and Society*. Philadelphia, Pennsylvania: Keith's Theatre Building. Vol. 1, No. 1. 13 March 1909. Weekly. [*Bulletin of Bibliography*, V (July 1909), 208.]

22. *Theater Shpigel und theater freind*. New York, New York. 20 February–7 May 1909. [In Yiddish. English Title: *Theatre Mirror and Theatre Friend*. The next entry is the English title.] NN

23. *The Theatre Mirror and Theatre Friend*. New York, New York: 119 East 92nd Street. Vol. 1, No. 1. February 1909. Weekly. In Hebrew. [*Bulletin of Bibliography*, V (April 1909), 178.]

1910

24. *Burlesque*. New York, New York: 1547 Broadway. Vol. 1, No. 1. 17 December 1910. Weekly. [*Bulletin of Bibliography*, VI (April 1911), 212.]

25. *Drama League of America*. Playgoing Committee Bulletin. New York, New York. Nos. 1-46. 20 September 1910–22 April 1913. Series 2. Nos. 1-18. 30 September 1913–28 April 1914. Irregular. DLC (1-40; Series 2, Nos. 1, 4, 6-11, 13-18), ICN (2-22, 24-40, 42-45), NN (1-30), OCl (Series 2, Nos. 4, 6-18)

26. *Drama League of America*. Chicago Center. Playgoing Committee. Bulletin. Chicago, Illinois. Nos. 2-45. 28 September 1910–15 April 1913. Irregular. [Inserted: Drama League of America announcements, 28 March and 4 May 1912.] ICN, NN (Nos. 2-30)

27. *Fair Topics*. Edited by E. Lloyd Sheldon. New York, New York: Pub-

lished Gratuitously for the Actors' Fund by *The Morning Telegraph*. Nos. 1-6. 9-14 May 1910. Daily. [I do not know if the 14 May issue is the final one.] NN

228. *The Foyer*. Des Moines, Iowa: 224 Second Street. Vol. 1, No. 1. 1 December 1910. Biweekly. [*Bulletin of Bibliography*, VI (April 1911), 212.]

229. *Ghosts*. A Magazine of Romance and Reason. Edited by Ernest Evangeline. Kansas City, Missouri: 203 Temple Block. Vol. 1, No. 1. February 1910. Semimonthly. NN

230. *Magic*. The Magazine of Wonder. Conducted by A. M. Wilson, M.D. Kansas City, Missouri: Published by Ernest Evangeline, 203 Temple Block. Vols. 1-3, No. 13. January 1910–April 1911. Monthly (irregular). [The numbering is continuous. Skips February 1910.] NN

231. *The Opera House Reporter*. Devoted to the Interests of Theatre Managers and the Theatrical Profession. A Live Wire in the Amusement World. Estherville, Iowa: James F. Cox & Co., Editors and Publishers. Vol. 12, No. 31–Vol. 21, No. 50. 11 November 1910–26 March 1920. Weekly. [Covers opera in all states.] NN (photostat copies; very imperfect collection)

232. *The Players Monthly*. New York, New York: 1 Madison Avenue. Vol. 1, No. 1. April 1910. Monthly. [Supposedly discontinued with No. 8, November 1910, but I have not been able to locate any of the numbers. *Bulletin of Bibliography*, VI (July 1910), 118; VII (April 1912), 14.]

1911

233. *Broadway Buzz*. New York, New York. Vol. 1, No. 1. April 1911. Monthly. [*Bulletin of Bibliography*, VI (October 1911), 276.]

234. *The Castle Square Program Magazine*. Castle Square Theatre. John Craig, Sole Lessee & Manager. An Illustrated Weekly Devoted to the Interests of The Castle Square Theatre and Its Patrons. Boston, Massachusetts. Vols. 1-2, No. 42. [In Vol. 1, there is a special issue between Nos. 13 and 14, dated 28 March 1911.] 2 January 1911–24 June 1912. Then, *The Castle Square Theatre Magazine*. Vols. 3-6, No. 42. 26 August 1912–19 June 1916. Weekly. [For at least a month each summer the magazine was not printed. In all, 246 issues. Distributed free at each performance.] MB

235. *The Daily Theatrical Herald*. Chicago, Illinois: 542 S. Dearborn Street. Vol. 1, No. 1. 1 June 1911. Daily. [*Bulletin of Bibliography*, VI (July 1911), 246.]

236. *The Drama*. A Review of the Allied Arts of the Theatre Sponsored by the Drama League of America and Published for All Interested in the Progress of the Stage. New York, New York: Drama Corp. Vols. 1-20. February 1911–May 1930. Then, *The Drama Magazine*. Chicago,

Illinois: Drama League of America. Vol. 21. June 1930–June 1931. Quarterly (February 1911–May 1919); monthly (October 1919–June 1924); eight numbers a year (October 1924–May 1930); nine numbers a year (October 1930–June 1931). [Absorbed the *Drama League Monthly* in 1919.] C, CSt, CtY, DLC, IC (to Vol. 20), ICN, ICU, IU, IaU, InU, MH, NIC, NN

37. *The Drama League of America, Bulletin*. Boston, Massachusetts. Nos. 1-94. August 1911–April 1918. Irregular. MB (missing Nos. 2, 33, 36, 39, 63, 87)

38. *In Stock*. A Monthly Magazine Devoted to Stock Plays, Managers, Authors and Players. Edited by Hoi Cooper Megrue. New York, New York: The American Play Company, Publishers, 1451 Broadway. Vol. 1, No. 1. February 1911. Monthly. NN

39. *M-U-M*. Magic, Unity, Might. The Society of American Magicians. Official Monthly Bulletin. New York, New York. Vols. 1-17. October 1911–1927. [Merged into and continued as a section of *Sphinx*.] DLC (1-[2]-[7-10]), NN (1-14)

40. *Theatrical Weekly Record*. New York, New York. Vol. 1, Nos. 1-41. 1911–3 September 1912. Then, *Theatrical Record*. To Vol. 2, No. 3. 10 September 1912–March 1913. Weekly. MH ([1-2])

41. *The Tip Folio*. New York, New York: Sanger and Jordan. Vols. 1-8. 1911–1917. Weekly. [Give information on plays presented by joint stock companies.] MH (incomplete)

42. *What's Going On in New York*. New York, New York. 20 March 1911–10 November 1913. Then, *What's Going On*. 17 November 1913–8 November 1915. Then, *What's Going On in New York*. 15 November 1915–29 May 1916. Then, *What's Going On*. New York's Social Calendar. 24 September 1916–28 May 1917. Then, *The Social Calendar*. 3 September 1917–16 May 1932. Weekly (omitting June–August). NN (incomplete)

1912

43. *The American Playwright*. A Monthly Magazine of Scientific Discussion of Plays and Playwriting. Edited by William Thompson Price. New York, New York: W. T. Price, 1440 Broadway. Vols. 1-4, No. 4. January 1912–15 May 1915. Monthly. [The final issue is one for April–May. Forty issues.] DLC, ICU, IU, MH, MiU, MnU, NN, OCl

44. *Drama League of America*. Washington Center. Bulletin of the Playgoing Committee, Washington Center of the Drama League, Washington, D.C. Nos. 1-41. 17 December 1912–15 February 1916. Monthly (irregular). [A broadside. Each is devoted to one play.] DLC

45. *The Dramatic Record and Guide*. Containing the Names and Achievements of All the Players on the New York Stage During the Year 1912,

Together with a Wealth of Information of Interest to All Theatre-Goers. New York, New York: The Dramatic Record and Guide Company, 1912. Annual. LU-M, NN

246. *The New Drama.* Boston, Massachusetts: 194 Boylston Street. Vol. 1, No. 1. April 1912. Biweekly. [*Bulletin of Bibliography*, VII (July 1912), 43; VII (October 1912), 70.]

247. *Stage Pictorial.* New York, New York: 1493 Broadway. Vol. 1, No. 1. March 1912. Monthly. [*Bulletin of Bibliography*, VII (July 1912), 43.]

1913 (See also *Theater un Muving Piktshurs*, Addenda, p. 86.)

248. *Century Opera Weekly.* New York, New York. Vol. 1, Nos. 1-7. 4 September–16 October 1913. Then, *Opera.* Vol. 1, Nos. 8-13. 23 October–27 November 1913. Weekly. DLC, NN

249. *The Conjuring Record.* Published Every Once-in-so-often by V. K. Allison. For Magicians, Illusionists, Ventriloquists, and Others of the Allied Arts. Bronxville, New York. Vols. 1-2, No. 12. 14 March 1913–February 1915.) Monthly (irregular). NN

250. *The Curtain Raiser.* New York, New York: Gaiety Theatre Building. Vol. 1, No. 1. March 1913. Monthly. [*Bulletin of Bibliography*, VII (July 1913), 142.]

251. *Drama League of America.* Bulletin of the Playgoing Committee of New York. New York, New York: 7 East 42nd Street. Nos. 1-57. 3 September 1913–12 March 1918. Irregular. [Broadside. The place of publication changes.] NN

252. *The Footlight.* Atlanta, Georgia: Empire Life Building. Vol. 1, No. 1. 18 January 1913. Weekly. [*Bulletin of Bibliography*, VII (October 1913), 163.]

253. *Foyer.* Edited by J. D. Wilson. Philadelphia, Pennsylvania: Stowell Publishing Co., 29 N. 13th Street. Vols. 1-3, No. 5. October 1913–March 1916. Monthly. DLC

254. *The Lantern.* Edited by C. J. Kirch. Chicago, Illinois: Lantern Publishing Co. Vols. 1-2, No. 4. 20 February–October 1913. Irregular. [Known as *The Saturday Night Lantern*, 22 March–20 May 1913.] NN

255. *Music Magazine and Musical Stage Review.* The National Music Weekly. Boston, Massachusetts. Vol. 1, Nos. 1-4. 15 February–8 March 1913. DLC, MB, MWA

256. *The Play-Book.* Edited by Thomas H. Dickinson. Madison, Wisconsin: Wisconsin Dramatic Society. Vols. 1-2, No. 12. April 1913–May 1915. Monthly. [Not published in April and May 1914.] CSt, DLC, IC, ICU, IaU, MnU, NN, PP, WHi, WM, WU

257. *Stage Quarterly.* New York, New York: 1493 Broadway. Vol. 1, No. 1. August 1913. Quarterly. [*Bulletin of Bibliography*, VII (October 1913), 164.]

58. *Vaudeville Year Book, 1913.* Published As a Compendium of General Information for the Vaudeville and Tabloid Field in the West and South. Chicago, Illinois: 820 Caxton Building. 1913. Then, *Vaudeville Year Book.* Representing the Field Covered by the Western Vaudeville Managers' Association. Chicago, Illinois: Vaudeville Year Book Company. 1914. Annual. MH (1914), NN (1913)

1914

59. *Bulletin of the Catholic Theatre Movement.* New York, New York. February 1914–3 April 1916. Then, *The Catholic Theatre Movement.* 19 May 1916–July 1932. Very irregular. DLC (incomplete), NN (incomplete; some sixty-two issues)

60. *Gus Hill's National Theatrical Directory.* Containing the Most Complete List of Theatres . . . for the United States and Canada . . . Information As to Towns . . . Railroads . . . Theatrical Managers . . . Plays . . . Vaudeville Theatres . . . Moving Picture Houses . . . Attorneys. New York, New York: Hill's National Theatrical Directory. 1914/15. DLC, NN

61. *International Music and Drama.* Edited by E. Valenti. New York, New York. Vols. 1-4, No. 23. 22 October 1914–July 1916. Weekly (irregular). NN

62. *The Little Review.* Literature, Drama, Music, Art. Edited by Margaret C. Anderson; with Jane Heap (1922-1929). Chicago, Illinois. Vols. 1-12, No. 2. March 1914–19 May 1929. Monthly (to April 1920); quarterly (irregular; May/June 1920–19 May 1929). [The subtitle varies.] CtY, DLC, ICU, NN (1-[5]-[7-8]-[10-12]), RPB

63. *Magical Bulletin of the Magical Shop of the West.* Edited by F. G. Thayer. Los Angeles, California: Issued by Thayer and Christianer. Vol. 1, Nos. 1-2. January–February 1914. Then, *Magical Bulletin of the Magical Shop of the West.* Official Organ of the Pacific Coast Society of Magicians. Vol. 1, No. 3–Vol. 12, No. 7. March 1914–May 1925. Monthly. [The subtitle changes.] MH ([1], 3-[4]-[8-9]), NN

64. *The Opera Magazine.* Devoted to the Higher Forms of Musical Art. [Edited by R. C. Penfield.] New York, New York. Vols. 1-3, No. 12. January 1914–December 1916. Monthly. DLC, ICN, MnM, NN, PP

1915

65. *Actors Bulletin.* Official Newsletter of the Actors' International Union. New York, New York: Actors' International Union, Columbia Theatre Bldg., Room 616, 7th Ave. and 47th Street. Vol. 1, No. 1. November 1915. [I have been unable to locate any additional information concerning this periodical.] DLC

266. *The Eagle Magician.* A Magazine Containing the Cream of Magic. By the Magician. For the Magician. Edited by Collins Pentz. Minneapolis, Minnesota: 1215 Nicollet Ave. Vols. 1-6, No. 11. 10 November 1915–June 1922. Monthly. NN

267. *Equity.* Official Organ of the Actors' Equity Association and the Chorus Equity Association. New York, New York. [The subtitle varies, as do the editors and the publication address.] Vol. 1–. December 1915–. Monthly. NN

268. *The Modern Stage Magazine.* Edited by Emanuel Reicher. New York, New York: Published by the Modern Stage, 1400 Broadway. Vol. 1, Nos. 1-2. November–December 1915. Monthly. [Emanuel Reicher was the director of the Modern Stage, a company which staged plays in 1915/16. He wanted it to be a repertoire company.] NN

269. *The New York Dramatic Chronicle.* Chronicling Theatrical Notes of Interest and List of Attractions at New York Theatres. New York, New York: Published by Frank V. Strauss & Company. Vols. 1-3, No. 9. 22 November 1915–14 January 1918. Weekly. [113 issues.] NN

1916

270. *The Cue.* Seattle, Washington: 4533 19th Street. Vol. 1, No. 1. 1916. Quarterly. [*Bulletin of Bibliography*, IX (July 1917), 173.]

271. *Drama League of America Monthly Bulletin.* Chicago, Illinois: Marquette Building. Vol. 1, No. 1. April 1916. Monthly. Then, *Drama League Monthly.* Mount Morris, Illinois: Published by the Drama League of America. Vol. 1, No. 2–Vol. 4, No. 1. September 1916–May 1919. Monthly (except June, July, August). [Merged into *Drama* and later *Drama Magazine.*] CtY, DLC, IEU, IEN, IU, IaU, InU, MB, MH ([1]-4), MWelC, NN, NvU, OC, WaU

272. *Drama League of America, Year Book—1915.* Based on the Addresses and Reports at the Fifth Annual Convention at Detroit, Comprising Valuable Contributions by Drama League Workers and Experts on the Vital Issues of the Day. Chicago, Illinois. 1916. Annual. DLC, NN

273. *The Escape Wizard.* Atlantic City, New Jersey: Chas. A. Bohem, Publisher, 104 S. Maryland Ave. Vol. 1, Nos. 1-3. 1 April–1 June 1916. Monthly. [No. 3 has the subtitle "A Magazine for Handcuff Kings & Magicians."] NN

274. *Holmes' Trade Sheet.* Edited by Donald Holmes. Kansas City, Missouri. Vol. 1, No. 1. November 1916. Then, *Holmes' Magical Notes and Comments.* Vol. 1, No. 2–Vol. 3, No. 12. December 1916–October 1920. Monthly (June 1917–November 1919; irregular). [Thirty-six issues.] NN

275. *The Outlaw.* "A Rascal and a Rogue in Many Ways, but Faithful to the

Theatre." Edited by Maurice Campbell. New York, New York: 381 Fourth Avenue. Vol. 1, Nos. 1-9. April–December 1916. Then, *The Outlaw. A Magazine of Comment and Criticism.* Vol. 2, Nos. 1-2. January–February 1917. Then, *The Outlaw. The New Era Magazine. Constructive Criticism of Current Happenings and Events.* Vol. 2, Nos. 3-4. March–April 1916. Monthly. NN

76. *Theatre Arts Magazine.* Detroit, Michigan: Society of Arts and Crafts. November 1916–December 1923. Then, *Theatre Arts Monthly.* January 1924–October 1939. Then, *Theatre Arts.* November 1939–January 1964. Quarterly (November 1916–October 1923); monthly (January 1924–January 1964). [From December 1917 to January 1964 published in New York City by Theatre Publications, Inc. Vols. 1-48, No. 1. November 1916–January 1964. An important magazine. Published plays also.] CtW, CU, ICR, ICU, IEN, IU, MH, MdBG, MiU, NIC, NN, NNC, OCl

1917

77. *The Little Theatre Magazine.* Edited by Adrian Metzger. San Francisco, California: Issued by The Players Club of San Francisco, 170 Second Street. Vol. 1, Nos. 1-2. May–June 1917. Then, *The Little Theatre Monthly.* Nos. 3-5. July–October/November 1917. Monthly (irregular). [Supersedes *Little Theatres.* Absorbed by *Drama.*] C, IU, NN (missing No. 1)

78. *The Magic World.* Edited by J. E. Pierce. Philadelphia, Pennsylvania: Published by the Magic World Publishing Company. Vols. 1-8, No. 1. April 1917–June 1924. Monthly (irregular). NN

79. *The Prompter. A Publicity Magazine Devoted to the Interests of Stock Managers.* Edited by J. J. White (8 September 1917–1 June 1918); Dewitt Newing (15–29 June 1918). New York, New York: Issued Semimonthly by Century Play Company, 1400 Broadway. Vols. 1-2, No. 13. 8 September 1917–29 June 1918. Semimonthly. [Twenty-two issues.] MH (missing Vol. 2, No. 1)

80. *Screen and Stage.* New York, New York: 263 Ninth Avenue. Vol. 1, No. 1. 26 May 1917. Biweekly. [*Bulletin of Bibliography*, IX (October 1917), 199.]

81. *Where and When.* New York, New York: 1416 Broadway. Vol. 1, No. 1. 15 January 1917. Weekly. [*Bulletin of Bibliography*, IX (April 1917), 147.]

1918

82. *Drama League Calendar.* New York, New York: New York Drama League, Inc., 7 East 42nd Street. Vol. 1, Nos. 1-15. 15 September

1918–15 April 1919. Biweekly. Then, *Drama Calendar*. Vols. 2-7, No. 30. 1 October 1919–27 April 1925. Then, *Drama Calendar*. A Weekly Guide to Theatrical and Musical Entertainment. Vols. 8-9, No. 35. 5 October 1925–30 May 1927. Weekly (October to May). Then, *The Drama Calendar*. An Organ of Opinion by and for Theatre Goers. Vol. 10, Nos. 1-28. 15 February 1928–1 January 1929. [Suspended 30 May 1927–15 February 1928. Vol. 2, No. 1 (October 1919), incorrectly called Vol. 1, No. 1. Edited by Henry Stillman (13 November 1922–7 April 1924, Vol. 5, No. 9–Vol. 6, No. 30); Theodore Fuchs (6 October 1924–27 April 1925, Vol. 7, Nos. 1-30); Frances Witherspoon (5 October 1925–23 November 1925, Vol. 8, Nos. 1-8); Gerald Ines Cutler (14 December 1925–8 February 1926, Vol. 8, Nos. 11-19); William W. Vogt (15 February 1926–30 May 1927, Vol. 8, No. 20–Vol. 9, No. 35); Margaret Wentworth (15 February 1928–1 January 1929, Vol. 10, Nos. 1-28). The place of publication changes.] DLC [1-7], IU (6-10), NN (2-[6]-[10]), OT (8-10)

283. *Plays and Players Pictorial*. New York, New York: 19 West 44th Street. Vol. 1, No. 1. 23 June 1918. [*Bulletin of Bibliography*, X (April/May/ June 1919), 112.]

1919

284. *Club Chatter and Dance Patter*. New York, New York. Vol. 1, Nos. 1-3. May–July 1919. Then, *Dance Review*. The Magazine for Dancers Everywhere. Vol. 1, No. 4–Vol. 2, No. 2. August 1919–March 1920. Monthly. DLC [1-2]

285. *The Coming Show*. New York, New York. Vol. 1, No. 1. November 1919. Monthly. [*Bulletin of Bibliography*, XI (May/August 1920), 32.]

286. *Critic*. An Authoritative Review of the Music World and Drama. Edited by Leila Chevalier. New York, New York: Chevalier Publishing Corp. Vol. 1, Nos. 1-5. June 1919–October 1920. Irregular. [November 1919 and February 1920 lack volume numbering.] NN

287. *Felsman's Magical Review*. Devoted to the Interests of the Magician and to Maintain the High Standards of Magic. Edited by Arthur T. Felsman. Chicago, Illinois: 115 S. State Street. Vols. 1-3, No. 1. October 1919–[October 1931 ?]. Monthly (irregular). [The final issue of Vol. 2 is dated November/December 1923. The New York Public Library dates Vol. 3, No. 1, as October 1931 ?] NN

288. *Shadowland*. Expressing the Arts. Edited by E. V. Brewster and others. Published by Brewster Publications, Inc. June 1920–1923. Jamaica, New York. October 1921–1923; Brooklyn, New York: The M. P. Publishing Company. Vols. 1-9, No. 2. 3 September 1919–October 1923.

Monthly. [Merged into *Classic*, November 1923.] CtY ([1-6]-9), DLC (missing Vol. 9, Nos. 1-2), NN ([3], 7-9), PP ([1], 4-9)

9. *The White Way Magazine.* Edited by M. B. Kleinfeld. New York, New York: Published by the Rialto Publishing Company, Inc., Atlas Building, 231–233 Tenth Avenue. Vol. 3, No. 7. September, 1919. Monthly. [I have not been able to discover any other issues.] NN (Vol. 3, No. 7)

1920

0. *Actor's Voice.* Los Angeles, California. Vol. 1, No. 1. January 1920. Monthly. [*Bulletin of Bibliography*, XI (May/August 1920), 32.]

1. *American Theatre.* New York, New York. Vol. 1, No. 1. September 1920. Monthly. [*Bulletin of Bibliography*, XI (January/April 1921), 68.]

2. *The Billboard's Index of New York Theatricals.* New York, New York. 1920/21. Annual. Then, *The Billboard Index of New York Theatricals.* 1921/22–1927/28. Then, *The Billboard Index of New York Legitimate Stage.* 1928/29–1936/37. Then, *The Billboard Year Book of the New York Legitimate Stage.* 1937/38. Then, *Facts and Figures on the New York Legitimate Stage.* 1938/39–1940/41. Annual. [1920/21–1930/31 issued as the special Fall number of *Billboard*.] MiD, NN

3. *Drama Brochure.* Waterloo, Iowa. Vol. 1, No. 1. April 1920. Monthly. [*Bulletin of Bibliography*, XI (May/August 1921), 90.]

4. *The Little Theatre Review.* Edited by M. Lacey-Baker, and Barbara Schelling. New York, New York: 713 Holland Building, Fifth Avenue. Vol. 1, No. 2. 4 November 1920. Biweekly. [I have not been able to locate the first issue. The second issue is to be located at Harvard University's Theatre collection in a box, "Printed Matter–N-Z."] MH

5. *Little Theatres.* Edited by S. Marion Tucker. New York, New York: Issued by the Little Theatre Service of the New York Drama League. Nos. 1-32. 15 November 1920–May/June 1924. Monthly (irregular). [No issues May–August 1921, May–August 1922, June–August 1923. November 1920, *Little Theatre Supplement.* Superseded by *Little Theatre News.* December 1920–April 1921 lack dates.] CU (1923–June 1924), DLC (March 1923–April 1923; September 1923–May/June 1924), NN

6. *New York Star.* National Vaudeville Artists; Vaudeville Managers Protective Association. New York, New York. Vols. 1-22, No. 8. 1920–27 December 1930. [The title varies, *Vaudeville News* (1920–March 1926), and then, *Vaudeville News and New York Star* (April 1926–8 June 1929)]. C ([3]-[7]), IU ([8-9]-[11]-[16-19]), NN ([1, 5, 12]-22), O ([8, 11])

7. *Play Mart.* New York, New York. Vol. 1, No. 1. January 1920. Irregular. [*Bulletin of Bibliography*, XI (September/December 1921), 108.]

298. *The Prompter.* Edited by Arthur Clyde. New York, New York: The Prompter Publishing Co., Inc. Vol. 1, Nos. 1-7. June–December 1920. Monthly. DLC, NN

299. *Rainbow.* Drama, Literature, Music, Art. Edited by Boris de Tanko and Horace Brodsky. New York, New York. Vol. 1, Nos. 1-3. October–December 1920. Monthly. CtY (Nos. 1, 3), ICU, NNMM

300. *The Stage.* A Monthly Magazine Devoted to the Profession and the Theatre-Going Public. Edited by James McLeod. Boston, Massachusetts: The Stage Publishing Company, 77 Church Street. Vols. 1-2, No. 14. 25 December 1920–February 1922. Monthly. [The dating is incorrect. Vol. 2, No. 5, is dated April 1922; Vol. 2, No. 6, is dated May 1922; Vol. 2, No. 7, is dated June 1922.] DLC

301. *Theatre World.* An Independent Weekly. Edited by J. J. O'Connor (24 January–24 April 1920); S. Jay Kaufman (1 May–4 October 1920). New York, New York: Published by Theatre World, Inc., 727 Seventh Avenue. Vols. 1-3, No. 11. 24 January–4 October 1920. Weekly. [Merged into *Dramatic Mirror* and continued as *Dramatic Mirror and Theatre World,* 16 October 1920.] NN (missing Vol. 2, Nos. 6-7, 9-13)

1921

302. *Cue* (Theta Alpha Phi). East Lansing, Michigan: Michigan State College. Vols. 1-34. 1921–1960. Bimonthly (during the school year). [It is difficult to obtain information about the periodical as copies seem to be very scarce. The title changed several times, e.g., *Cue of Theta Alpha Phi.* Publication seems to have been suspended from Summer 1941 to Fall 1946 (Vol. 20, No. 3–Vol. 22, No. 1). Published three times a year from 1955. Published later in Terre Haute, Indiana, and in Chicago, Illinois.] DLC (incomplete), NN (incomplete), WyU (incomplete)

303. *Music Record and Opera News.* New York, New York: J. Wanamaker. Vols. 1-3. March 1921–May 1924. Monthly (irregular). [Supersedes *Opera News.*] NN (1-[2-3])

304. *Pantomime.* New York, New York: World Building. Vols. 1-2, No. 11. 28 September 1921–18 March 1922. Weekly. NN ([1-2])

305. *The Play List.* A Practical Guide to New and Standard Plays of Interest to Little Theatres. Edited by S. M. Tucker (February 1921–April 1924). New York, New York. Nos. 1-38. January 1921–October 1925. Monthly (September–April, slightly irregular). [Typewritten sheets, January 1921–March 1923. Nos. 23-30 (September 1923–April 1924) issued by the Little Theatre Service of New York Drama League. November 1924–May/October 1925 were issued as a part of *Little Theatre Month-*

ly, under the caption, *The Little Theatre Play List.* No. 1, January 1921, has the title *Monthly Play List.*] NN

6. *The Playlist of the New York Drama League.* Edited by S. Marion Tucker. New York, New York: Issued by the Little Theatre Service of the New York Drama League, East 42nd Street. Nos. 1-30. January 1921–April 1924. Monthly (from September to April). [Mimeographed, Nos. 1-22. January 1921–April 1923. Printed, Nos. 23-30. September 1923–April 1924.] NN

7. *Washington Play-goer's Weekly.* Washington, D.C. Vol. 1, No. 1. 10 December 1921. Weekly. [*Bulletin of Bibliography,* XI (May/August 1922), 148.]

8. *Zit's Weekly.* New York, New York. Vols. 1-33, No. 17. 1921–8 May 1937. [*Zit's Theatrical Weekly.* December 1935–May 1937. Suspended 7 December 1932–7 January 1933.] NN ([19]-33)

1922

9. *Bulletin of the Outdoor Players of Peterborough, N.H.* Boston, Massachusetts: Pierce Building, Copley Square. Vol. 1, No. 2. May 1922. Quarterly. [I found this one issue in the Harvard University Library Theatre Collection in a box marked "Printed Matter–N-Z."] MH (only the one issue, No. 2, May 1922)

0. *The New York Dramatic Chroncile.* New York, New York: Issued Fortnightly by the New York Theatre Program Corporation, 108-114 Woster Street. Vols. 1-4, No. 18. 27 November 1922–1 October 1926. Biweekly. [Ninety issues.] NN

1. *Shubert Theatre News.* Boston, Massachusetts, Vol. 1, No. 1. 13–18 February 1922. MB

2. *Theatre and School.* Berkeley, California. Vols. 1-15, No. 4 1922–May 1937. Monthly (October to May, April 1926–May 1932); four times a year (October 1932–May 1937). [Official Publication of the Drama Teachers' Association, April 1926–May 1937. Vol. 15 is mimeographed. Subtitle varies.] C (missing Vols. 1-3), CSt, CU (6-15), NN ([4]-15)

1923

3. *Dance Lovers Magazine.* New York, New York. Vols. 1-5, No. 2. November 1923–December 1925. Then, *Dance Magazine.* Vol. 5, No. 3– Vol. 17, No. 2. January 1926–December 1931. Monthly. DLC, NN ([1]-[5]-[10]-17)

4. *Idishe musikalishe welt un teater zshurnal.* [*Jewish Musical World and Theatre Magazine.*] New York, New York. Vol. 1, Nos. 1-2. March– September 1923. Irregular. NN

5. *Theatre Guild Bulletin.* [First edited by Lawrence Langnor, then by

Hiram Motherell.] New York, New York. Vols. 1-2. December 1923–
November 1925. Then, *Theatre Guild Quarterly*. Vols. 3-5. December
1925–September 1928. Then, *Theatre Guild Magazine*. Vols. 6-9, No.
7. October 1928–April 1932. Then, *The Stage*. The Magazine of After
Dark Entertainment. Vol. 9, No. 8–Vol. 16, No. 11. May 1932–June
1939. Monthly, quarterly, irregular. DLC (6-16), IC (incomplete),
NcU (2-16), NN ([2-5]-16), NPV ([1-2]-14)

316. *The Theatrical Herald*. Edited by J. E. Lewis. San Francisco, California:
J. E. Lewis, Publisher. The Theatrical Herald, Room 421 Liberty Bank
Building, 948 Market Street. [Address for 2 and 9 June numbers was
607-9 Pantages Bldg.] Vol. 1, Nos. 1-11. 3 March–9 June 1923. Weekly. C-S

1924

317. *Chicago and Mid-West Musicians' Directory*. With Dramatic and Dancing
Arts. Chicago, Illinois: Midwest Concert. 1924/25. [I have not been
able to discover any other editions.] NN

318. *Denishawn Magazine*. A Quarterly Review Devoted to the Art of the
Dance. New York, New York. Vol. 1, Nos. 1-4. 1924–1925. Quarterly.
DLC, MoS, NN, OCl, PP, WaS

319. *The Drama Yearbook, 1924*. Edited by Joseph Lawren. New York, New
York: Joseph Lawren. Annual. CtY, DLC, MH, MiU, NN

320. *Footlight and Lamplight*. A Weekly Review of Plays and Books Broadcast
from Gimbel Brothers. By Oliver M. Sayler. New York, New York:
W. G. B. S. Vol. 1, No. 1. 30 October 1924. [Broadside sheet.] MH

321. *Greenwich Playbill*. A Leaflet Issued with Each New Production at the
Greenwich Village Theatre-Season 1924-1925. New York, New York.
Nos. 1-[6]. 1924/25–1925/26. Irregular. NN

322. *Jewish Theatrical News*. Devoted to Progress in the Amusement World.
Edited by Aaron Singer. New York, New York: The Jewish Theatrical
News, 1493 Broadway. Vols. 1-2, No. 20. [Twenty-six issues.] 1 October 1924–29 June 1926. Monthly (Vol. 1, 1 October 1924–May 1925).
[Not published January and February 1925.] Weekly (9 February–
29 June 1926). [Not published June 1925–2 February 1926.] DLC
(1-[2]), NN (missing No. 15), NNJ ([1])

323. *The Little Theatre Monthly*. Edited by S. M. Tucker. New York, New
York: Published by the Little Theatre Service of the New York Drama
League, Inc., 29 West 47th Street. Vol. 1, Nos. 1-7. November 1924–
May 1925. Monthly. [Supersedes *Little Theatres*. Absorbed by *The
Drama Magazine*.] CSt, CU, NN, PU, Tx, TxDaM

324. *The Little Theatre News*. Edited by S. M. Tucker. New York, New York:
Published by the Little Theatre Service of the New York Drama League,
Inc., 29 West 47th Street. Vol. 1, Nos. 1-28. 18 October 1924–27 April

1925. Weekly. [*Little Theatre News* and *Little Theatre Monthly* combined with *Drama* October 1925. Supersedes *Little Theatres.*] CtY, CU, IU, NN, PP

25. *The Little Theatre Play List*. New York, New York: New York Drama League. November 1924–October 1925. Monthly (irregular). NN (incomplete)

26. *Melbourne's Magazine of Plays and Players*. New York, New York: Published by G. Townsend Melbourne, 145 West 45th Street. Summer 1924. Quarterly. [Each issue was to contain illustrated stories of eight or more plays "conceded to be the successful New York Productions of the Period."] NN

27. *New York Amusements*. Broadway's Theatre Guide. New York, New York: Published by New York Amusements Publishing Company, 250 West 54th Street. Vol. 2, No. 18–Vol. 18, No. 3. 21 January 1924–14 January 1939. Weekly. [I have not been able to discover any issues before Vol. 2, No. 18. The subtitle varies.] NN

28. *Players Magazine*. Edited by Donald M. Kastler (November 1924–October 1929); Anna Best Joder (November/December 1929–May 1945). Lawrence, Kansas, National Collegiate Players (November/December 1924–November/December 1936). Then, *Players Magazine*. The National Journal of Educational Dramatics. January/February 1937–December 1940. Then, *Players Magazine*. Representing the Educational Theatre in America. January 1941–May 1945. Then, *Players Magazine*. Serving the Educational Theatre. Edited by Clark Weaver (? November/December 1945–May 1961). November/December 1945–[April?] 1950. Then, *Players Magazine*. Serving the Theatre and Related Fields. May 1950–February 1953. Then, *Players Magazine*. Serving the Needs of Those in Theatre. March 1953–May 1960. Then, *Players Magazine*. Serving Directors, Teachers, Students of Theatre, and Related Fields Since 1924. October 1960–May 1961. Then, *Players Magazine*. Serving Theatres Across America. (Edited by Gordon Beck). October 1961–. [The last issue at the University of Wisconsin, according to the librarian's letter in the spring of 1966, is Vol. 42, No. 4, Spring–Summer 1966. Vol. 43 was slated for publication in the fall of 1967, but under new management.] Quarterly (during the school year, 1924–June 1931); five times (during the school year, September 1931–June 1935); six times (during the school year, September 1935–August 1939); eight times (during the school year, October 1939–.) [Place of publication varies. Reprinted, Vols. 1-20, 1920–1944, AMS Press catalogue, 1968.] ICU, MH, MiU, NN, WU (lacks Vol. 32, No. 1, October 1945)

29. *The Shakespeare Association of America Bulletin*. New York, New York. Vols. 1-24, No. 4. June 1924–October 1949. Annual (1924–1926); three issues a year (1927–1928); quarterly (1929–1949). [Superseded by

Shakespeare Quarterly. Reprinted, AMS Press catalogue, 1968.] CLSU, CU, CtY, ICN, ICU, IEN, MH, MiU, NN, NjP, OCIW, PP, TxU, ViU, WaU

330. *Theatre and Drama.* Issued Monthly. New York, New York: 132 West 43rd Street. Vol. 1, No. 11. May 1924. Monthly. [I have not been able to locate any other issues.] NN (Vol. 1, No. 11)

1925

331. *Actors Directory and Stage Manual.* Edited by Murray Phillips. New York, New York: Philrose Publishing Co., 160 W. 46th Street. Vols. 1-2, No. 2. June 1925–April 1926. [April 1926 issue is called a supplement.] Irregular. DLC, NN

332. *The Continental Theatre.* New York, New York: Continental Theatrical Information Service, 145 West 45th Street. Vol. 2, No. 24–Vol. 4, No. 10. 20 June 1925–6 March 1926. Weekly. [The New York Public Library catalogue says that this is a sample periodical, not completely catalogued. Mimeographed.] NN (missing all before Vol. 2, No. 24)

333. *The Intimate Theatre.* Edited by Ernest V. Heyn and Harry Steeger. Princeton, New Jersey: Princeton Théâtre Intime. Vol. 1, Nos. 1-2. February–April 1925. Three issues a year. [Published under the auspices of the Intimate Theatre at Princeton University.] NjP

334. *New York Theatrical Business Men's Guide.* New York, New York: Compiled and Published by H. P. Hanaford, 1400 Broadway. 1925–27. Annual. NN (1925, 1927)

335. *Pasadena Community Playhouse News.* Pasadena, California: Pasadena Playhouse Association, 39 South El Molino Avenue. October 1925–May 1933. Then, *Pasadena Playhouse News.* 1933–12 June 1946. [August 1941 was the last issue to have volume and number. Vols. 1-20, No. 2.] Irregular. [The University of Southern California lists the run as twenty-one volumes. The New York Public Library lists an issue for 29 October 1947.] CLSU (incomplete), CtY (incomplete) NN (very incomplete)

336. *The Playbill of Alpha Psi Omega and Delta Psi Omega.* October 1925–1929. Then, *The Playbill of Alpha Psi Omega* [after 1929 *The Playbill of Delta Psi Omega* was issued separately]. Edited by Paul F. Opp (1925-1934); Arthur Hammel (1935-1938); Paul F. Opp (1940-1967); Donald Garner (1968–). Fairmont, West Virginia: Fairmont Printing Press, The Fraternity Press, University Avenue, St. Paul, Minnesota. 1929–. Annual. [Dr. Paul Opp supplied some of the information in a letter. The publication is "published annually by the Alpha Psi Omega Dramatic Fraternity."] NN (missing, 1938, 1940, 1944-1946, 1949, 1960–.)

337. *The Professional Bulletin for Producers, Managers, Directors and Artists.*

Edited by H. H. Wentworth. New York, New York: Service Bulletin, Inc., 500 Fifth Avenue. Vol. 1, No. 1. May 1925. Then, *The Professional Bulletin.* Stage and Screen. Vol. 1, Nos. 2-5. July 1925–February 1926. Irregular. [February 1926 dated on the cover January 1926.] NN

338. *The Professional Stage and Screen Bulletin.* New York, New York: 424 Thirty-third Street. Vol. 1, No. 1. November 1925. [*Bulletin of Bibliography,* XII (May/August 1926), 199. This seems to be the same periodical as the preceding.]

339. *The Repertory Spectator.* Boston, Massachusetts: Published by The Jewett Repertory Theatre Fund, Inc., 264 Huntington Avenue. Vol. 1, Nos. 1-12. April 1925–March 1926. Monthly. [Free.] MB, MH (missing No. 12), NN

340. *Show World.* The Blue Book of Show Land. New York, New York: The Show World Publishing Company. Vols. 1-7, No. 3. 1925–18 February 1928. Semimonthly. NN ([2-7])

341. *Stage and Foyer.* New York, New York: 225 West 34th Street. Vol. 1, No. 1. November 1925. Monthly. [*Bulletin of Bibliography,* XII (May/ August 1926), 199.]

342. *Stage and Screen.* The Magazine for Everybody. Edited by Frank Armer, and Jack Edwards. New York, New York: Published by Ramer Reviews, Inc., 104 West 42nd Street. Vols. 1-2, No. 5. December 1925– December 1926. Monthly (irregular.) [Vol. 2, No. 3, never published. The place of publication changes.] NN

343. *The TPROA Quill.* The Press Agent's Paper. Published Periodically. New York, New York: The Theatrical Press Representatives of America, Inc., 1400 Broadway. Vols. 1-10, No. 5. 1925–May 1934. Monthly (irregular). [Vol. 4 has two issues numbered 4.] NN (1-[6-8]-10, on film), PP (2-10)

1926

344. *The Playgoer.* A Magazine for the Theatre. Edited by A. L. Weeks (1926-?); John D. Williams (24 March 1947–23 May 1949); Hazel A. Bruce (5 September 1949–9 May 1954). Detroit, Michigan: Theatre Program Co., 321 Lafayette Blvd. Vols. 1-54. 5 September 1926–9 May 1954. Weekly (during the theater season). [Vol. 6, 1931–1932, not published as the *Playgoer* but as a series of miscellaneous programs.] MiD (Vol. 7 is incomplete)

1927

345. *American Dancer.* New York, New York. Vols. 1-15, No. 3. June 1927– January 1942. Then, *American Dancer* combined with *Dance.* Vol. 15, Nos. 4-5. March–April 1942. Then, *Dance* combined with *American*

Dancer. Vol. 15, Nos. 6-9. May–August 1942. [No issue was published February 1942. There are errors in numbering the volumes.] KyU, MdBE, MnS, NN ([1-3]-15), PP (1-15)

346. *Church and Drama Bulletin.* Edited by Margaret Wentworth (24 September 1929–10 June 1930); Omar Pancoast Goslin and Ryllis Clair Alexander (5 November 1930–7 January 1931). New York, New York: Issued by Church and Drama Association, 105 East 22nd Street. Vols. 1-3, No. 39. 27 September 1927–10 June 1930. Then, *Mask and Chancel. The Sign of The Chapel Guild and the Best in Drama.* Vol. 4, Nos. 1-10. 5 November 1930–7 January 1931. Weekly (September–June). [128 issues.] NN, NR ([3]-4), PP ([1-4])

347. *Journal of Expression.* Edited by Martin Luther. Lynn, Massachusetts: Expression Company, Publishers, 113 Market Street. Vols. 1-6, No. 2. [Twenty-two issues.] June 1927–April 1932. Quarterly. DLC, IEN, KU, MnU, NBuG, NN, OOxM, PP, WU

348. *The Little Theatre of Dallas Magazine.* Dallas, Texas: The Little Theatre of Dallas, 2019 Bryan Street. ["Published with each production at the Little Theatre of Dallas."] Vols. 1-14. [190 issues.] October 1927–May 1943. Monthly (from October to May, with irregularities). [The magazine contained a listing of costs and a newsletter concerning the activities of the theater group.] NN (Vols. 1-9, No. 2), TxDa (incomplete; missing about twenty issues)

349. *The Log of the Little Theatre.* Denver Community Players. Denver, Colorado. Nos. 1–. October 1927–. [Gohdes, p. 33.]

350. *The Scenic Artist.* Official Organ of the United Scenic Artists Association. New York, New York. May 1927–April 1928. Monthly. [These are the only issues about which I have any information.] NN

351. *The Vigilant.* A Journal of Opinion Published the Tenth of Every Month. Edited by H. Z. Torres. New York, New York: The Vigilant Company, 1 West 81st Street. Vol. 1, Nos. 1-2. 15 March–15 April 1927. Monthly. NN

1928

352. *Amateur Dramatic Year Book and Community Theatre Handbook, 1928-1929.* Edited by G. W. Bishop. New York, New York: Macmillan Co., 1928. Annual.

353. *The Carolina Play-Book.* Of The Carolina Playmakers and the Carolina Dramatic Association. Edited by Frederick Koch. Chapel Hill, North Carolina: Published at the University of North Carolina, by The Carolina Playmakers and The Carolina Dramatic Association. Vols. 1-17. March 1928–December 1944. Quarterly. [Supplement, *The Carolina Stage,* 1936-1944.] CtY, DLC, FU, GU, MH, MiU, NN, NPV, NcGW, NcU, NjP, OClW, PBL, PU

54. *Footlights and Kliegs.* Chicago, Illinois: 3011 N. Nagle Avenue. Vol. 1, No. 1. October 1928. Monthly. [Supposed to have changed to *Footlights and Shadows* with Vol. 2, No. 1, December 1929, but I have been unable to locate any issues. See *Bulletin of Bibliography*, XIV (January/April 1931), 87, 88.]

55. *Fortnightly Musical Review.* New York, New York. Vols. 1-2, No. 3. 4 January–28 November 1928. Semimonthly. [No numbers issued for July and September.] DLC, NN

56. *The Official Theatrical World of Colored Artists.* National Directory and Guide. Authentic Information of Musicians, Concert Artists, Actors, Actresses, Performers and All Others Allied with the Professions. New York, New York: The Theatrical World Publishing Company. 1928. Semiannual. DLC

57. *Theatre News.* New York, New York. Vols. 1-4, Nos. 1-17. 1928–16 April 1932. Weekly (irregular). NN ([2-4])

1929

58. *The Circus Scrap Book.* Edited by F. P. Pitzer. Jersey City, New Jersey: 41 Woodlawn Avenue. Vol. 1, Nos. 1-16. January 1929–October 1932. Quarterly. [Nos. 1-4 also called Vol. 1.] NN

59. *The Drama Service Bulletin.* Edited by Bruce Carpenter. New York, New York: Prentice-Hall, Inc., 70 Fifth Avenue. Nos. 1-4. November 1929–May 1930. ["Published four times each theatrical season: November, January, March, and May."] CL, NBuG, NN (missing Nos. 1 and 3)

60. *Harlequinade.* Abilene, Texas. Vols. 1-2, No. 2. 15 October 1929–June 1930. Semimonthly (irregular). [Mimeographed.] NN

61. *High School Thespian.* National Thespian Dramatic Honor Society for High Schools. Cincinnati, Ohio. Vols. 1-16. 1929–May 1944. Eight times a year. Then, *Dramatics.* The Educational Magazine for Directors, Teachers and Students of Dramatic Arts. Cincinnati, Ohio: National Thespian Society, College Hill Station. Vol. 17–. 1945–. [Amateur theatricals.] DLC (missing Vols. 1-3), NN (missing Vols. 1-5)

62. *Parade.* A Magazine of Music–Theatre–Allied Arts. Edited by Robert Faber. New York, New York: Published by the D-H-B Publishing Company, Inc., 150 West 46th Street. Vol. 1, Nos. 1-2. August–September 1929. Monthly. NN

63. *The Playbill of Delta Psi Omega.* Edited by Paul F. Opp (1929-1934); Arthur Hommell (1935-1941); Paul F. Opp (1942-1967); Donald R. Garner (1968–). Fairmont, West Virginia: Box 347; The Fraternity Press, University Avenue, St. Paul, Minnesota. October 1929–. Annual. [Before 1929 this was part of *The Playbill of Alpha Psi Omega and Delta Psi Omega.* Because of this, care must be taken in regard to the

volume numbers, as Vols. 1-3 are called Vols. 4-6.] NN (missing 1938, 1940)

364. *Rob Wagner's Beverly Hills Script.* Edited by Rob Wagner (1929–August 1942; with Florence Wagner, 8 October 1938–1 August 1942); Florence Wagner (15 August 1942). Beverly Hills, California: Wagner-Lynds Co., Vols. 1-12; Wagner Publishing Co., Vol. 13–Vol. 33, No. 751; Associated Publishers, Inc., Los Angeles, Vol. 32, No. 752–Vol. 35, No. 775. Vol. 1–Vol. 35, No. 775. 16 February 1929–March 1949. [Vol. 28 omitted in numbering.] Title becomes *Script*, Vol. 32, No. 722–Vol. 35, No. 775. 2 February 1946–March 1949. Weekly (1929–13 November 1937); forty-five times a year (20 November 1937–11 October 1941); biweekly (23 October 1941–March 1949). CLU, CU, NN

365. *The Show-Goer.* Seattle, Washington. Vol. 3, Nos. 14-17, 21-22, 24-27. 13 March–3 April, 1–8 May, 12–22 June 1929. [I have been unable to locate any other information concerning this periodical.] NN

366. *Stage Stories.* New York, New York: 100 Fifth Avenue. Vol. 1, No. 1. February 1929. Monthly. [*Bulletin of Bibliography*, XIII (January/April 1929), 163.]

367. *Theatre 1929.* A Magazine Published by the New Playwrights Theatre. Edited by Bernard Smith. New York, New York: 133 West 14th Street. Vol. 1, Nos. [1]-2. December 1928–January 1929. Monthly. MH

1930 (See also *The Players Bulletin*, Addenda, p. 86.)

368. *The Civic Repertory Theatre Bulletin.* Edited by Mollie B. Steinberg. New York, New York: Published by the Civic Repertory Theatre, Inc., 105 West 14th Street. Vol. 1, No. 1. October 1930. Then, *The Civic Repertory Theatre Magazine.* Vol. 1, Nos. 2-8. November 1930–May 1931. Monthly. [Each issue has an essay on the history of the 14th Street Theatre.] DLC, MH, NN, PU

369. *Dancers Club News.* New York, New York: Published by the Dancers Club. [1930?] 24 December 1931–May 1932. Then, *The Dance World.* August 1932. Monthly (irregular). [Vols. 1-3, No. 7. 1930–August 1932.] NN (missing all before 24 December 1931)

370. *The Olympian.* Monthly Bulletin of the Los Angeles County Drama Association. Edited by Virginia Dahl (1931-1934). Glendale, California: Published by the Los Angeles Drama Association. Vols. 1-2, No. 4. 1930–March 1932. Then, *Little Theatre Magazine.* Edited by Elizabeth Clauss (1934-1935). Vol. 2, No. 5–Vol. 5, No. 3. April 1932–March 1935. Monthly (with some variations). [Forty-seven issues.] CL, CLSU (2-5), DLC ([1]-[3]-5), NN (missing all before Vol. 2, No. 12)

371. *The Prompter of the Mount Vernon Community Players, Inc.* Mount Vernon, New York. Vol. 6, No. 1–Vol. 8, No. 5. September 1930–June 1933. Irregular. [Sixteen issues. Edited by George L. Pendleton (Sep-

tember 1930–June 1931); Genevieve H. Cheney (October 1931–June 1933). I have not been able to locate any issues before Vol. 6.] NN
72. *Puppetry.* A Yearbook of Puppets & Marionettes. [The subtitle varies.] Edited by Paul McPharlin. [Printed variously in Birmingham, Michigan, Detroit, Michigan, and New York.] Published by the Marionette Fellowship of America. Vols. 1-16. 1930–1946/47. Annual. [I do not know if any volumes were printed between 1942 and 1944.] MiD (missing all before 1934, 1935–1940, 1941–1944), NN (missing 1942–1944, 1946)
73. *Shakespeare Studies.* New York, New York: Shakespeare Association of America. Nos. 1-3. 1930–1932. Irregular. [No. 1 reprinted, with additions from the association's *Bulletin*, Vol. 5, No. 2.] CSt, LNHT, MH
74. *Theatre Engineering Building and Maintenance.* Edited by R. W. Baremore. New York, New York: Theatre Engineering, Inc., 45 West 45th Street [later, 7 West 44th Street]. Vols. 1-3, No. 4. May 1930–August 1931. Monthly. [Devoted mainly to movie theaters. Combined with *Moving Picture Review* and *Theatre Management*, September 1931.] NN ([1]-3)

1931

75. *Call Board.* Official Organ of Catholic Actors Guild of America. New York, New York: Hotel Astor [later, Hotel Knickerbocker, and then Hotel Piccadilly, 227 W. 45th Street]. Vol. 1–. December 1931–. Monthly (except July-August); bimonthly (October-June). Irregular. NN (incomplete)
76. *Lagniappe.* For All Those Who Are Interested in the Amateur Stage. Evanston, Illinois: Published by the Dramatics Department of Row, Peterson & Company, 1911 Ridge Avenue. Vols. 1-31, No. 3. October 1931–1 January 1962. Irregular (from three to six issues a year). NN
77. *Practical Stage Work.* Current Plays for Little Theatres. Briggsville, Wisconsin: Catholic Dramatic Movement. Nos. 1-3. 1931/32–1932/33. Annual. NN
78. *Scenic Artist News.* Report of the Little Theatre Committee, United Scenic Artists Association. New York, New York. Vols. 1-2, No. 3. April–August 1931. Monthly. NN
79. *The Seven Circles.* The Official Publication of the International Magic Circle. Edited by Walter B. Gibson (April 1931–February 1934); J. N. Hilliard (March–June 1934). Three Rivers, Michigan: Published by the International Magic Circle. Vols. 1-5, No. 6. April 1931–September 1934. Monthly. [Published in Three Rivers, Michigan, Kalamazoo, Michigan, and Odessa, Missouri.] DLC (1-5), NN (1-[3-4]), TxU (1-5)
80. *Silver Falcon.* New York, New York: Published by the Shakespeare So-

ciety of Hunter College of the City of New York. [Nos. 1-5?] 1931–1936. Semiannual; annual. [Fall 1931 and Spring 1931, 1934, 1935, and 1936. I have not been able to locate any other issues.] NN

381. *Today's Plays of New York*. The Magazine That Knows the Shows. Published for the Patrons of the Public Service Theatre Ticket Office. New York, New York: Published by Today's Plays Publishing Company. Vol. 1, 1-13. 5 January–30 March 1931. Weekly. NN (missing Nos. 11-12)

382. *Worker's Theatre*. New York, New York: Published by the Workers Laboratory Theatre, Section of the Workers International Relief Culture Activities Department. Vols. 1-3, No. 8. April 1931–August 1933. Monthly. [Mimeographed Nos. 7-8 (July–August 1933), are called Vol. 5 instead of Vol. 3. Printing began with Vol. 2 (April 1932). Superseded by *New Theatre*.] MH, NN (very incomplete), WM ([2-5])

1932 (See also *Virginia Drama News*, Addenda, p. 87.)

383. *Broadway Chorus*. New York, New York: 114 West 26th Street. Vol. 1, No. 1. 30 November 1932. [*Bulletin of Bibliography*, XV (May/August, 1933), 15.]

384. *Cue*. The Magazine of Stage and Screen. New York, New York: Cue Publishing Co., 20 W. 43rd Street. Vol. 1–. 1932–. Weekly. [The subtitle varies. Place of publication changes.] CL, DLC (missing Vols. 1-3), ICU (missing Vols. 1-3), MH (missing Vols. 1-4), NN (missing Vol. 1)

385. *The Dragon*. Official Organ of the I.S.J.M. Edited by Vernon E. Lux. Mount Morris, Illinois: Published by the International Society of Junior Magicians. Vols. 1-15, No. 2. September 1932–September 1946. Monthly (irregular). NN

386. *Lambs Script*. New York, New York: Published by the Lambs Club. Vols. 1-24. January 1932–September/October 1955; 1956–December 1959; March/April–September/October 1960. Then, a new series. Vol. 1, Nos. 1-7. 1 April–1 August 1961. Edited by Cy Mann. Holiday issue, 1962. Edited by Ed. Weiner. Monthly (slightly irregular), 1932-1943; irregular, 1944–1961 (biweekly, Nos. 1-5; monthly, Nos. 6-7). [Publication suspended December 1932–September 1933; February 1934–February 1935; November 1935–March 1936; September/October 1956–holiday issue, 1957/58. There are many errors in numbering, between 1932 and 1955; three issues, October 1933, January 1934, and March 1935, are called Vol. 2, No. 1. Vol. 6, No. 1 (January 1939), is incorrectly dated 1938. The new series is mimeographed. Superseded by *Script*.] NN and Lambs Club in New York

387. *Mummery*. New York, New York: 853 Broadway. Vol. 1, No. 1. March,

1932. Monthly. [*Bulletin of Bibliography*, XIV (May/August 1932), 181.]

88. *Slapstick*. New York, New York: 570 Seventh Avenue. Vol. 1, No. 1. February 1932. Monthly. [*Bulletin of Bibliography*, XIV (January/April 1932), 161.]

89. *Ultra Magical Review*. New Haven, Connecticut: Petrie-Lewis Mfg. Co., Inc., Westville Station. Vol. 1, No. 1. March 1932. NN

1933

90. *Broadway Follies*. New York, New York: 1472 Broadway. Vol. 1, No. 1. July 1933. [*Bulletin of Bibliography*, XV (September/December 1933), 35.]

91. *The Iowa Play Production Festival*. University of Iowa Extension Bulletin. Iowa City, Iowa. 1933–1955. Annual. NN (incomplete, fifteen numbers)

92. *Little Theatres of the South Magazine*. New Orleans, Louisiana: Medical Building. Vols. 1-3. August 1933–June/July 1936. Monthly (irregular). DLC, LU ([1-3]), TxH ([2-3])

93. *The N.V.A. News*. For Artist, Manager, Agent and All Those Connected with Stage, Screen, and Radio. The Official Organ of the National Variety Artists, Inc. Edited by Mark Vance. New York, New York: 229 West 46th Street. Vol. 1, Nos. 1-37. 21 April–30 December 1933. Weekly. [Vol. 1, Nos. 14-15 (21–28 July 1933) called Vol. 1, No. 15-15a.] NN (missing No. 34)

94. *Playhouse*. Boston and New England Show Review. Boston, Massachusetts. Vols. 1-3. 25 March 1933–7 October 1935. Weekly. [The subtitle varies.] MH ([2-3])

1934

95. *Four Arts*. A Monthly Journal for Artists and Art Appreciators. [Title varies: *4 Arts*, *IV Arts*. The drama editor was Norman Felton.] Cleveland, Ohio: Published at 1857 E. 63rd Street to February 1935, then at 6709 Euclid Avenue. Vol. 1, Nos. 1-11. April 1934–April 1935. Monthly (except July and August). NN ([1934]-1935), NNMM, OCl

96. *The Jinx*. An Independent Monthly for Magicians. Waverly, New York: Published by Theo. Annemann. Nos. 1-151. October 1934–December 1941. Monthly. [Superseded by *Phoenix*.] MH, NN

97. *New Theatre*. A Magazine of Drama, Film, Dance. Organ of the Workers Theatres of U.S.A. (Section of the International Union of Revolutionary Theatre) and Workers Dance League. Edited by Herbert Kline; then, Ben Blake. New York, New York: Published by the New Theatre League, and the New Dance League, with the National Film and

Photo League, 42 East 12th Street. Vols. 1-3, No. 11. January 1934–
November 1936. Then, *New Theatre and Film.* Vol. 4, Nos. 1-2.
March–April 1937. Monthly (irregular). [Suspended December 1936–
February 1937. Supersedes *Workers Theatre.* Vol. 1, Nos. 6-7 (June–
July/August 1934), lack volume numbering. Vol. 1, Nos. 1-5 (January–
May 1934), called Vol. 3, Nos. 2-6, in continuation of the volume num-
bering of *Workers Theatre.* Absorbed *Filmfront,* April 1935. Mimeo-
graphed. Harvard University has the first issue, dated September/Oc-
tober 1933.] CU, MH, MiU, NN, NBuG

1935

398. *American Gilbert and Sullivan Quarterly.* New York, New York: American Gilbert and Sullivan Association. Spring 1935–Spring 1938. Quarterly. DLC ([1935–1938]), MH (1935–[1936–1938]), NN ([1935–
1936]), NNR (1935–[1936–1938])
399. *Aria.* New York, New York: Published by the Grand Opera Artists' Association of America. Vols. 1-3, No. 1. October 1935–January/February
1937. Irregular. [Vol. 1 is complete in one issue. In Vol. 2, Nos. 3-10
were never published.] DLC (missing all after Vol. 1), MdBE, NN
(1-[2]-3)
400. *Charles T. Jordan Series of Magical Effects.* Waverly, New York. Nos.
1-6. November 1935–April 1936. Monthly. NN
401. *Federal Theatre.* Bulletin of the Federal Theatre Project . . . A Division
of the United States Works Progress Administration. Edited by Pierre
de Rohan. New York, New York: Issued by the Bureau of Research
and Publication for All Workers on the Federal Theatre Project, 701
Eighth Avenue. Vols. 1-2, No. 5. 25 November 1935–14 June 1937,
with a special number for May 1938. Monthly. [Mimeographed. Two
No. 4 issues in Vol. 2.] CtY, ICN (1-[2]), ICU (missing Vol. 1, Nos.
7-12), MH ([1-2]), MdBE, NB, NN, NNQ, NPV, OCl
402. *Handy Green Book Directory of the Theatre Industry of New York.* An
Amazingly Useful Guide and Contact Medium for Everyone Interested
in the Theatre. New York, New York: Compiled and Published by
Handy Green Book Publishing Co., 214 West 42nd Street. Vols. 1-10,
[12 Nos.] Fall 1935–Spring 1941. Two issues a year. [The title varies
slightly.] NN
403. *Theatre Events.* "Special Issue." [New York, New York? No. 1.] 25
May–1 June 1935. [No date, editor, city of publication, or publisher
is given. Mimeographed. The issue is devoted to National Theatre
Week, 25 May–1 June 1935.] NN
404. *Theatre News.* News and Comments on All Forms of Entertainment for
the New Haven Area. Edited by Jack W. Schaefer. New Haven, Con-

necticut: Theatre Patrons, Inc. Vols. 1-12, No. 19. 16 May 1935–7 November 1940. Weekly. [Title changes: *New Haven Theatre News*; *New Haven County Theatre News*. Reviews movies more than plays.] CtY (missing Vol. 1, No. 3)

1936

05. *The Carolina Stage*. A Supplement to the Carolina Play-Book. Edited by John W. Parker. Chapel Hill, North Carolina: Published by the Carolina Dramatic Association at the University of North Carolina. Vols. 1-9, No. 2. March 1936–December 1944. Irregular. [Mimeographed. No issues published in 1941 and 1943. Vol. 9 was edited by Virginia Page Spencer.] CtY (missing all after May 1940), DLC, ICU (incomplete), MH, NN, PU (1-8)

06. *Centre Aisle*. A New and Distinctive Magazine of the Theatre. Edited by M. W. Loppnow (February 1936–April 1937); with Mark Markson (February–June 1936); Thomas Arthur and William Merle (18 December 1940–29 April 1942). St. Paul, Minnesota: 141 East 5th Street. Vol. 1, Nos. 1-4. February 1936–May 1936. Then, *Centre Aisle*. A Journal of the Non-Professional Theatre. [Subtitle varies.] Vol. 1, No. 5–Vol. 5, No. 12. June 1936–11 June 1943. Monthly (February 1936–1 April 1937, with no issues during January and February 1937); Weekly (irregular), 18 December 1940–11 June 1943. [The magazine suspended publication with Vol. 2, No. 1 (26 April 1937). From 9 March to 7 December? 1940 it appeared as a weekly column in the *St. Paul Herald*. It resumed separate publication with Vol. 2, No. 41 (18 December 1940).] DLC (missing Vol. 1), NN (incomplete, missing Vol. 1, Nos. 2-3; Vol. 4, Nos. 47-52; Vol. 5, No. 9), MnHi

07. *The Drama*. Edited by Garrett H. Leverton, and Ralph Denis. Evanston, Illinois: Northwestern University Drama Service Guild. Vols. 1-2, No. 3. [Nos. 1-8.] 14 September 1936–14 April 1938. Irregular. CtY, IEN, MnU

08. *Genii*. The Conjuror's Magazine. Los Angeles, California: Genii Publishing Co., 929 Longwood Ave. 1936. Monthly. [*Standard Periodical Directory*, 306.]

09. *Little Theatre News*. New York, New York: Published in the Interest of the Y.W.C.A. Little Theatre Group, Central Branch, Y.W.C.A., 53rd Street and Lexington Avenue. Vols. 1-3, No. 2. [Eighteen issues.] April 1936–February/March 1938. Monthly (except for summer months, when there were no issues). [Mimeographed. Superseded by *Scene*, October 1938.] NN (missing Vol. 1, Nos. 1-2)

10. *Major Bowes Amateur Magazine*. Edited by Henri Weiner. New York, New York: Published by Andrews Publishing Company, 220 West 42nd Street. Vol. 1, Nos. 1-4. March–June 1936. Monthly. NN

411. *Opera News.* New York, New York: Metropolitan Opera Guild, Inc., 654 Madison Avenue. Vol. 1–. December 1936–. Weekly (during the opera season); biweekly (spring and fall). ICN ([1-9]+), MB (4+), MdBE (4+), NN, NR (3+)

412. *Theatre Workshop.* A Quarterly Journal of the Theatre and Film Arts. An Official Publication of the New Theatre League. Edited by Mark Marvin. New York, New York: New Theatre League. 117 W. 46th Street. Vols. 1-2, No. 1. October/December 1936–April/June 1938. Quarterly (irregular). CtY, DLC, ICU, IEN, IaU, MH, MWC, MoK, NBuG, NN, OCl, PPV, PU

413. *The Tops.* An Independent Magazine of Magic. Colon, Michigan: Abbott's Magic Novelty Company. Vols. 1-22, No. 3. January 1936–March 1957. Monthly. [Official Organ of the Magician's Guild of America, May 1938–December 1941. Subtitle varies.] DLC (1-19), NN (missing Vol. 16, No. 4)

1937

414. *The Arts Quarterly.* New Orleans, Louisiana: Published at Dillard University. Edited by Randolph Edmonds and Frederick Hall (1937); Randolph Edmonds, Rudolph Moses, Frederick Hall, and Charlotte Crawford (1938); Charlotte Crawford (1939). Vols. 1-2, No. 4. April/June 1937–December 1939. Quarterly. LNHT (missing two issues), LU, NN, NjR

415. *Catholic Theatre Conference Bulletin.* Washington, D.C. Vol. 1, Nos. 1-4. 1937–May 1938. Then, *Catholic Theatre.* Vol. 2, Nos. 1-3. November 1938–January 1940. Irregular. [Suspended February 1940–May 1941.] New Series, June 1941–. KAS (2+), MBtS

416. *Curtain Call.* A Publication of the National Office of the New Theatre League. New York, New York: 132 W. 43rd Street. [October 1937?] Monthly. [Mimeographed. The year 1937 is mentioned on p. 7. The editor says that the magazine has appeared in the past.] NN

417. *The Grapevine Telegraph of the Puppeteers of America.* A News-Sheet Published from Time to Time for Members. Edited by Paul McPharlin (to No. 31, March/April 1944); Marjorie Batchelder (from No. 32, May/June 1944). Birmingham, Michigan. Nos. 1-44. November 1937–February 1947. Irregular (to 1940); bimonthly (1941–June 1949). [Publication suspended March 1947–August 1948.] Then, *The Grapevine.* Published by the Puppeteers of America. Edited by George Latshaw. [Nos. 1-6.] September 1948–June 1949. Bimonthly (irregular). [Superseded by *Puppetry Journal* after June 1949.] NN

418. *Little Theatre Arts.* Edited by Charles H. Connelley. St. Louis, Missouri: Little Theatre Arts Publishing Co., 204 Mid-City Building. Vol. 1, No.

1. February 1937. Monthly (except July-August). [*Bulletin of Bibliography*, XVI (May/August 1937), 55.]

19. *One Act Play Magazine*. Edited by William Kozlenko (May 1937–February 1941); S. Emerson Golden (March/April 1941–May/June 1942). New York, New York: Published by the Contemporary Play Publications at 112 West 42nd Street. Vols. 1-2, No. 8. May 1937–February 1939. Monthly (irregular). Then, *One Act Play Magazine and Theatre Review*. Vol. 3, Nos. 1-7. January–November/December 1940. Bimonthly (from No. 3, March/April 1940). Then, *One Act Play Magazine and Radio-Drama Review*. Vols. 4-5, No. 3. January/February 1941–May/June 1942. Bimonthly (March/April 1940–May/June 1942). [Merged into *Plays*. The Drama Magazine for Young People. Suspended March–December 1939.] DLC, ICU, IEN, KU, MB, MH, MiD, NN, NjP, OCl, PU

1938

20. *The Actor*. San Francisco, California: 324 Hyde Street. Vol. 1, No. 1. March 1938. Monthly. [*Bulletin of Bibliography*, XVI (May/August 1939), 183.]

21. *Bulletin of the Dramatists' Assembly*. Stanford, California: Issued by the Dramatists' Alliance of Stanford University. 1938–1948. Annual. [Mimeographed.] IEN (1940-), NN, PSC, TN

22. *The Catholic Theatre Year Book*. [Edited by Mathias Helfen.] Oconomowoc, Wisconsin. Published by the Catholic Dramatic Movement. Vols. 1-5. 1938/39–1942/43. Annual. [Issue for 1938/39 is mimeographed. From 1939/40 the work is printed. Volume for 1939/40 was issued instead of Vol. 11, Nos. 1-2, of *Practical Stage Work*.] DLC, NN

23. *Chamberlain Brown's Theatre Record*. Edited by Jack H. Seligman. New York, New York: Published by Chamberlain Brown, 145 W. 45th Street. Vol. 1, Nos. 1-2. 7 June 1938–[?] 1938. Irregular. Then, *Theatre Record News*. A Newspaper Devoted to the Best Interests of the Theatre. Vol. 1, No. 3-[?]. 9 December 1938–26 May 1939. Irregular. [Mimeographed.] NN (7 June, 9 December 1938; 23, 24, 30, and 31 March 1939; 22, 23, 24, 25, and 26 May 1939)

24. *Contemporary Scene*. A Play Quarterly. Edited by Albert Prentis. New York, New York: Published by the China Aid Council in Cooperation with the Cultural Department of the American League for Peace and Democracy, New York City Division, 112 East 19th Street. Vol. 1, No. 2. Summer 1938. [Mimeographed. I have not been able to locate the first issue.] Quarterly. NN (missing No. 1)

25. *The Continental Theatre*. Edited by Pierre de Rohan (Nos. 4-6). New York, New York. Compiled by the National Service Bureau, Federal

Theatre Project, Works Progress Administration. [Vol. 1], Nos. 1-3. October–December 1938. Monthly. Then, *The Theatre Abroad*. A Monthly Review of the Stage in Other Lands. Vol. 1, [Nos. 4-6]. January–May 1939. Monthly (irregular). [Mimeographed. January–May 1939 issued without series title or numbering.] IEN (missing No. 4), NN, NNC (missing Nos. 4, 6)

426. *The Curtain Rises*. Monthly Magazine of the Chicago Drama League. A Review of the Allied Arts of the Theatre Sponsored by the Chicago Drama League and Published Ten Times a Year for Those Interested in the Progress of the Stage. Edited by Leonard Bridges (October 1938–April 1939); Irene Mansfield Affleek (June 1939–November 1939). Chicago, Illinois: Chicago Drama League, 415 South Michigan Ave. Vols. 1-2, No. 7. October 1938–April 1940. Monthly (October to June). Irregular. [The size changed with Vol. 1, No. 4 (January 1939), and Vol. 2, No. 7 (April 1940)]. IC (to November 1939), NN (missing Vol. 1, No. 7, and Vol. 2, Nos. 4-6)

427. *Dramatis Personae*. Chronicle of the American Theatre. Organ of the unrecognized but promising American Playwright. Edited by Michael Trent. Port Washington, Wisconsin. Vols. 1-2, No. 2. [Spring] 1938–Summer 1939. Quarterly. [Published unpublished plays. Each number contains a play by Michael Trent.] NN

428. *The Negro Actor*. Official Organ of the Negro Actors Guild of America, Inc. Edited by Geraldyn Dismond (Vols. 1-2, No. 2); Edward G. Perry (Vol. 2, No. 3). New York, New York: 1674 Broadway. Vols. 1-2, No. 3. [Seven issues.] 15 July 1938–14 February 1940. Quarterly. [Superseded by *Negro Actor's Guild of America, Inc., Newsletter*.] MH, NN, NjP

429. *New Theatre News*. Edited by Mark Marvin, John E. Bonn, Ben Irwin, Alice Evans. New York, New York: Published by the New Theatre League, 132 W. 43rd Street. Vol. 1, Nos. [1]-3. [November?] 1938–January/February 1939. [Printed.] Then, *New Theatre News*. Information Service and Bulletin of the New Theatre League, 110 West 47th Street. Edited by Ben Irwin. Vol. 1, No. 4–Vol. 2, No. 2. November 1939–October 1940. Then, *New Theatre News*. Official Organ of the New Theatre League. Vol. 2, Nos. 3-4. November–December 1940. Then, *New Theatre News*. Information Service and Bulletin of the New Theatre League. Vol. 2, Nos. 5-11. January–June/July 1941. [Mimeographed. Suspended publication March–October 1939.] NN ([1]-2), NPV ([1]-2)

430. *Non-professional Drama Calendar*. New York, New York. Vol. 1, Nos. 1-7. December 1938–June 1939. Monthly. [Amateur theatricals.] NN

431. *The Play Shop*. A Magazine for the Amateur Producer and Actor. Published as an Extension Project of the Division of Dramatics of the Penn-

sylvania State College. State College, Pennsylvania. Vol. 1, No. 4–
Vol. 13, No. 2. January 1938–June 1952. Four issues a year (irregular).
[Mimeographed. I have not located the first three issues.] DLC

2. *The Puppet-Tree.* [Ottawa, Illinois]: Published by the Junior Puppeteers
of America. No. 1. November 1938. [Mimeographed.] NN

3. *Scene.* The News Organ of the Little Theatre Group, Central Branch
YWCA. Edited by Frances C. Rogers (October 1938–October 1939);
Ann Korall (November 1939–May/June 1940). New York, New York.
Vols. 1-2, No. 7. 28 October 1938–May/June 1940. Monthly (irregu-
lar). [Fifteen issues. Occasional issues lack dates. Vol. 1, Nos. 1-4
(October 1938–January 1939) lack titles. Mimeographed. Supersedes
Little Theatre News.] NN

4. *School and Theatre.* Edited by Harold J. Kennedy. New York, New
York: Published by the Theatre Education League, 1430 Broadway.
Nos. 1-3. November [1938]–[June 1939]. Irregular. [The 1939 issues
are undated and lack periodical title and numbering.] NN

5. *Stage Practice.* Published Occasionally by Dramatists Play Service, Inc.
Established by Members of the Dramatists Guild of the Authors League
of America for the Handling of the Nonprofessional Acting Rights of
Members' Plays and the Encouragement of the Nonprofessional Theatre. Edited by Henning Helms. Houston, Texas: 707 Chelsea Boulevard. Nos. 1-9. December 1938–February 1942. Irregular. [The
second issue lists the place of publication as New York, New York: 6
East 39th Street. Suspended publication during the war, with No. 9.]
IdU (4+), NN, OrU (2-9), TxU (1, 3+)

6. *TAC.* Issued by Theatre Arts Committee. Edited by Edno Ocko. New
York, New York: Published Monthly by Theatre Arts Committee, 132
West 43rd Street. July–October 1938. Then, *TAC.* November–Decem-
ber 1938. Then, *TAC.* Theatre, Film, Dance, Radio, Music. January
1939. Then, *TAC Magazine.* Theatre, Film, Dance, Radio, Music.
February–December 1939. Then, *TAC.* Stage, Screen, Radio, Dance,
Music. 15 February 1940–August 1940. [Vols. 1-2.] Monthly (slightly
irregular). MdBE (1-[2]), NN (1-[2]), NPV ([1]-2), NjP (1-2),
NjR (1-2)

7. *Theatre Library Association Report.* New York, New York. 1938. Then,
Annual Report. 1939–1940. Then, *Report of the Secretary.* 1941. Then,
Secretary's Report. 1942. Then, *Annual Report of the Secretary.* 1943.
Annual. NN

8. *Universal Blue Book.* The Who's Who of the Screen, Stage, Radio and
Television. New York, New York. Vol. 1. Fall 1938. [I have not been
able to locate any later issues.] NN

1939

439. *Bandwagon.* Circus Historical Society, Inc. Columbus, Ohio: Circus Historical Society, Inc. 2515 Dorset Road. 1939. Monthly. [*Standard Periodical Directory*, p. 305.]

440. *Callboard.* A Little Newspaper for the Little Theatre. Official Organ of the Drama Federation of America. Edited by Geoffrey Whalen. Chicago, Illinois: Published by Whalen and Carmack, 139 N. Clark Street. Vol. 1, Nos. 1-5. March–August/September 1939. Monthly (irregular). NN

441. *The Community Theatre Cue.* Edited by Newton Hoyt. South Bend, Indiana: Published by the Community Theatre, 316 South Chapin Street. Nos. 1-24. December 1939–23 April 1943. Irregular. [Changed size with No. 20. 23 October 1942.] NN (missing No. 23)

442. *Drama Educators of America, Inc., Official Bulletin.* New York, New York. Vols. 1-3, No. 6. 1939–July/August 1941. Irregular. NN ([3])

443. *4A Actors News.* Official Publication of Associated Actors and Artists of America an International Union. Hollywood, California. Vol. 1, Nos. 1-2. 11-18 September 1939. Weekly. [Also a New York edition.] NN

444. *Info about New York.* Edited by Jerry Askwith. New York, New York: Info, Inc. Vol. 1, Nos. 1-46. 17 March 1939–12/26 April 1940. Weekly (17 March–22 December 1939); biweekly (16 February–26 April 1940). [No issues 29 December 1939–9 February 1940.] NN

445. *Little Theatres of Southern California.* Bulletin Issued Monthly by the Riverside Community Players. Edited by Esther E. Brown. Riverside, California. [1939?]–[1941 or 1942?] Monthly (from September to June). Mimeographed. [Mrs. Thompson (Esther Brown), in a letter to Elma Marvin, corresponding secretary of the Riverside Community Players, is our only source of information about the magazine. She said that no copies were kept as far as she knows. The purpose was to keep Little Theatre Groups in Southern California informed of each others' activities.]

446. *The Luntanne Tatler.* [Official Newspaper of the Lunt-Fontanne Company, Appearing in "There Shall Be No Night," a New Play by Robert E. Sherwood at the Alvin Theatre.] Edited by Bob Downing. New York, New York. Vol. 1, No. 6–Vol. 3, No. 1. 5 November 1939–14 September 1940. Weekly (irregular). [Mimeographed. I have not been able to locate Vol. 1, Nos. 1-5.] NN (missing Vol. 1, Nos. 1-5)

447. *Manhattan.* By Night–by the Week–by Day. New York, New York: Kent Publications, Inc. Vol. 1, Nos. 1-15. 26 January–6 May 1939. Weekly. NN

448. *National Theatre Conference.* Quarterly Bulletin. A Co-Operative Organization of Directors of Community and University Theatres Organized Collectively to Serve the Non-Commercial Theatre. Cleveland,

Ohio: Western Reserve University. Vols. 1-12, No. 4. [Forty-five issues.] April 1939–December 1950. Quarterly. [Vols. 1-5, 1939–1943,
as Quarterly Bulletin.] DLC, MB, MdBE, MiD, MoS, NN, NR, NhU,
OCl, PP, TxH

49. *News-letter.* The Shakespeare Fellowship, American Branch. New York,
New York: The Fellowship, 17 E. 48th Street. Vols. 1-4. December
1939–October 1943. Bimonthly. Then, *Shakespeare Fellowship Quarterly.* Vols. 5-9, No. 2. January 1944–Summer 1948. Quarterly. [42
issues.] CoU, CtY, ICU, IaU, MH, MnU, NN, NjP, OU, WaU

50. *Theatre Arts Signpost.* New York, New York: Published by Theatre Arts
Monthly, 40 East 49th Street. Vols. 1-3, No. 4. January 1939–November 1941. Monthly (irregular). [Many issues are not dated.] DLC
(1-3), NN, ViU (1-2)

1940

51. *Actors' News.* Official Publication of American Guild of Variety Artists,
Branch of 4A's, Affiliated American Federation of Labor. Edited by
Edward Harrison. New York, New York: 2 West 45th Street. [Branch
of Associated Actors and Actresses of America.] Vol. 1, Nos. 1-12. 16
March–October 1940. Biweekly (16 March–6 July 1940); monthly
(August–October 1940). NN

52. *American Theatre Magazine.* Edited by Albert McCleery. New York,
New York: 2 East 46th Street. Vol. 1, No. 1. March 1940. Monthly.
NN (10th Avenue branch)

53. *Asides.* An Informal Publication Devoted to Articles, Study-Lists, and
General Critical Comment upon Drama and the Related Arts. Stanford,
California: Issued by the Dramatists Alliance. Vols. 1-3. 1940–1942.
Quarterly. Vols. 4-7. 1943–1948. Annual; biennial. [Mimeographed.]
CSt, CU, CoU, IEN, MB, MH, MiD, MiU, NN, NjP, PSC, WU

54. *Broadside.* Edited by Sarah Chokla Gross. New York, New York: Published by the Theatre Library Association, 476 Fifth Avenue. Vols. 1–
24, No. 1. May 1940–Fall 1963. Very irregular. [Varies from one to
six issues in a year.] CtY, DLC, MiU (1940–1958), NN, PU

55. *Conjurer's Chatter.* A Newsletter Published Now and Then by the Conjurer's Shop. Edited by Stuart Robson. New York, New York: 324
West 56th Street. Vol. 1, Nos. 1-27. [?] 1940–February 1947. Irregular. [The subtitle varies slightly. I do not know the date of the first
issue, but the second issue was published in October 1940.] DLC
(2, 4), NN (missing No. 1)

56. *Critics' Theatre Reviews.* New York, New York: Critics' Theatre Reviews,
Inc., 150 E. 35th Street. Vol. 1. 27 May 1940–1942. Then, *New York
Theatre Critics' Reviews.* 8 February 1943–. Weekly (except summer).
[Reprints reviews of plays as given in the various New York papers.]

CU, CoDU, CtY, IC, ICU, IEN, IU, MB, MH, MnM, MoU, NB, NN (missing Vol. 1), NcU, NjP, OOxM, OU, PP, TxU

457. *Dance*. New York, New York. Vol. 1, Nos. 1-3. January–March 1940. Monthly. DLC

458. *The Drama Leaguer*. Wilmington, Delaware: Published by the Drama League, P. O. Box 504. January 1940–[November 1943]. Irregular. [Broadside to June 1941.] NN (incomplete; nineteen issues. During the latter part of 1941 and during 1942 and 1943 the issues are not dated.)

459. *Dramatic Newsletter*. Edited by Will MacDonald and Robert Muniz. New York, New York: 600 W. 169th Street. Vol. 1, No. 1. 15 November 1940. [Biweekly? Mimeographed. On Little Theatres and Community Players in New York.] NN

460. *Music Makers*. Covering the Popular Music Field. Edited by Lyle K. Engel. New York, New York: The Music Makers, Inc. Vol. 1, Nos. 1-2. May–September 1940. Then, *Music Makers of Stage, Screen, Radio*. Vol. 1, No. 3. December 1940. Bimonthly (irregular). DLC, NBuG, NN (film)

461. *Negro Actors of America, Inc., Newsletter*. New York, New York. Vols. 1-3. May 1940–December 1943. Monthly (irregular). [Mimeographed. Vol. 1, No. 4, missing. June–December 1943 called Vol. 2, Nos. 2-5. Nos. 4 and 5 are repeated. May 1942–March 1943 does not have numbered issues.] DLC (incomplete), NjP, NN

462. *Opera*. Official Publication of the Musical Retreat Club, Inc. Edited by Mario Girardon. New York, New York. Vol. 1, Nos. 1-7. March 1940–April 1941. NN

463. *Prologue*. A Journal for Amateur and Community Theatres. Edited by Will MacDonald and Robert M. Muniz. New York, New York: Will MacDonald, 600 West 169th Street. No. 1. December 1940. Monthly. [Mimeographed. The editors say that this issue introduces a new format and a new name. Formerly the magazine was known as the *Dramatic Newsletter*. Treats mostly of the stage in New York.] NN

464. *Short Hauls*. Official Publication of Dexter Fellows Tent, Circus, Saints & Sinners Club of America, Inc. Edited by F. P. Pitzer. New York, New York: 22 East 40th Street. Vol. 2, No. 2–Vol. 8, No. 5. January 1940–May 1944. Monthly. [There are also two issues for January and May 1957 at the New York Public Library. I have not been able to discover any issues before Vol. 2, No. 2.] NN

465. *Stage*. Edited by Alexander King. New York, New York: Ince Publishing Company, 7 East 44th Street. Vol. 1, Nos. 1-4. November 1940–February 1941. Monthly. CtY, DLC, IC, ICU, IEN, IU, IaU, KAS, MB, MH, MiU, NIC, NjP, OU, PP, TN

466. *Theatre Review*. Bay Head, New Jersey. No. 1. 1940. [*Union List of*

Serials lists the magazine at Brown University. Miss Christine D. Hathaway, Brown University librarian, says that the library does not have a copy of the magazine. I have been unable to discover any additional information.]

1941

67. *AETA News.* Issued by the American Educational Theatre Association. Brooklyn, New York: Speech Department, Brooklyn College. Vols. 1-7, No. 1. 1941–January 1948. [Mimeographed.] Urbana, Illinois: University of Illinois. Vol. 7, Nos. 2-9. February 1948–January 1949. Ann Arbor, Michigan. Vol. 8, Nos. 1-9. February–December 1949. Vols. 1-8, No. 9. 1941–December 1949. Monthly (except July–September, with combined issue for May/June). [The magazine changed size with Vol. 8, No. 1.] CLSU (7-8), CST ([5, 7]-8), NN (Vols. 6-8, No. 9)

68. *Actor's Cue.* Published for and by Actors and Playwrights. Edited by Leo Shull. New York, New York: 128 West 48th Street [later, Hotel St. James, 111 West 4th Street]. Vols. 1-8, No. 22. [Volume and issue not given until Vol. 7, No. 25, 1 July 1947.] 30 September 1941–1 June 1948. Daily (except Saturday and Sunday, with variations, to December 1945); weekly (from 1 January 1946). Mimeographed. [Title varies from time to time. *Actor's Cues,* 13 October 1941; *Actors Cues,* 21 October 1941; *Genius Inc.,* 12 May 1942; *Actors Cues,* 18 May 1942; *Genius Inc.,* 20 May 1942; *Actors Cues,* 21 May 1942. Combined with *Daily Theatre,* 16 October 1945. Beginning 8 April 1947, *Actors Cues. The Entertainment Newsweekly.* 5 August 1947, drops volume and number, and does not resume them until 20 April 1948. Vol. 8, No. 16, an "Anniversary Issue," appears in 1948. Beginning 8 April 1947, the magazine is printed. There are a number of errors in dating, e.g., 29 April 1942 should be 30 April 1942; 21 September 1942 should be 22 September 1942. Various issues lack dates. January 1942 issue called an annual. Continued as *Show Business.*] NN

69. *Almanac.* Designers, Scenic Artists, Studio Operators, Make-up Artists, Costume Designers, Mural Artists Guild, Diorama, Model Maker and Display-Artists. Classified Directory. New York, New York. 1940/41. Annual. NN

70. *Bandwagon.* Circus Historical Society. Farmington, Michigan. [November?] 1941–June 1947. [November? 1941–December 1945 called Vols. 1-4. Absorbed by *Hobby-Swapper,* later *Handy Bandwagon.*] MWA (2-4), NN ([1941]-1947)

71. *Border Light.* Austin, Texas: Issued by the University of Texas Curtain Club. The Department of Drama. The College of Fine Arts. Vol. 1,

Nos. 1-4. 15 October 1941–23 April 1942. Irregular. [Mimeographed.]
NN

472. *Directory of Music.* Entertainment, Drama, for Buffalo and Niagara Frontier. Buffalo, New York. 1941–. [Gohdes, p. 150.]

473. *The Gallery of Stars.* The First Issue of the Lambs Own Magazine. Edited by William C. Lengel. New York, New York. Vol. 1, No. 1. Winter 1941/42. Semiannual. [This is the only issue I have been able to locate.] DLC

474. *The Handbook Annual of the Theatre.* Edited by Wilbur Dingwell. New York, New York: Coward-McCann, Inc. [Vol. 1.] 1940/41. Annual. [A comprehensive review of the New York theatrical season.] CL, CtY, DLC, ICU, MB, MnU, NN, NNC, OCl, TxU, WU

475. *"Lest We Forget."* Curtain Falls on Notable Theatrical Personages. Paul E. Glace. Reading, Pennsylvania: Embassy Theatre. 1941–1953/54. Annual. [Devoted to those actors, etc., who died during the last year. The volumes discovered are for 1941–1942, 1944–1948, 1950–1953/54 (called 17th season).] MH

476. *Plays.* The Drama Magazine for Young People. Boston, Massachusetts: Published by Plays, Inc., 8 Arlington Street. Vol. 1–. September 1941–. Monthly (September through June, with irregularities). [Absorbed *One Act Play Magazine*, October 1942. Amateur theatricals. The last issue I have seen is Vol. 25, No. 4, January 1966.] CL, DLC, ICU, MH, MdBJ, NBuG, NN, OU, TxU, WaU

477. *Revue.* News of the Theatre. Edited by Roberta Fauber. St. Louis, Missouri: 5628 Clemens Street. Vol. 2, No. 1. 8 February 1941. [I have not been able to locate any other issues.] MH (Vol. 2, No. 1)

478. *Show Business.* The Entertainment Weekly. Edited by Ira Bilowit. New York, New York: Leo Shull Publications, 155 West 46th Street [later, 136 West 44th Street]. Vols. 1-24, No. 33. 1941–15 August 1964. Weekly. [For earlier file, whose numbering it continues, see *Actors Cues*, 1941.] DLC, NN ([8-11]+)

479. *Straw Hats.* New Haven, Connecticut: P. O. Box 360. Vol. 1, Nos. 1-10. 20 June–22 August 1941. Weekly. [Suspended publication 22 August–16 October 1941.] Then, *Diversion*. The Amusement Weekly. Vols. 2-3, No. 21. 16 October 1941–14 May 1942. Weekly. [Forty-one issues.] CtY (missing Vol. 3, Nos. 1, 5, 11, 15, 18)

480. *Summer Theatre Directory.* Edited by Claire Shull. New York, New York: Leo Shull Publications, 136 W. 44th Street. 1941. Semiannual. [*Standard Periodical Directory*, p. 865.]

1942

481. *The Catholic Theatregoer.* Detroit, Michigan: The Catholic Theatre of Detroit. [Program of the Detroit Catholic Theatre.] Vols. 1-10. Oc-

tober 1942–January 1954. [Vol. 1, No. 6, May 1943 cancelled.] Irregular. [The date of April 1954 given as closing date is incorrect, as the April date is the last issue of *The Children's Stage.*] MiD

82. *Dramatic Center News.* Newark, Delaware: University of Delaware Dramatic Center. Vols. 1-26, [Nos. 1-91?]. [Vols. 1-26 constitute the entire issue of the magazine. The title given above is for October 1942–September 1948.] Then, *Delaware Dramatic Center News.* October 1948–January 1966. Irregular. [Mimeographed. C. Robert Kase was director of the Dramatic Center until 1966, and his name appeared at the head of each issue. Publication was suspended January 1943–September 1945. Also known as *University Dramatic Center News Bulletin.*] DeU (incomplete)

83. *The Theatre Annual.* New York, New York: Theatre Library Association. [Vols. 15-20 in Cleveland, Ohio, at Western Reserve University.] Vols. [1]–20. 1942–1963. Annual. [Vols. for 1942–1947 lack numbering, but constitute Vols. 1-6. Publication suspended between Vol. 14, 1956 (published 1956), and Vol. 15, 1957/58.] CU, DLC, IU, MH, MiD, MiU, NIC, NN, NjP, OU, PPi, PU, TN, ViU, WU

1943

84. *Hugard's Magic Monthly.* Devoted Solely to the Interests of Magic and Magicians. Edited by Jean Hugard. Brooklyn, New York: 2621 East 27th Street. Vols. 1-20. No. 12. June 1943–August 1963. Monthly. [The editors change, as does the place of publication.] DLC (1-[4]-[7]), NN

85. *Teater Heftn.* [Also *Theatre Leaves.*] New York, New York: Hebrew Actors Union of America. Nos. 1-11. 1943–1947. Irregular. [In Yiddish.] BM, MH (1-2, 5, 10-11), NN

86. *The Theatre Book of the Year.* A Record and Interpretation. By George Jean Nathan. New York: A. Knopf. Vols. 1-9. 1942/43–1950/51. Annual. AzU, CLU, CU, DLC, IEN, MdBE, MoU, NN, NNC, NjP, OCl, PU, RPB, TN

87. *Two Masques.* Devoted to a Better Theatre and Motion Picture. Edited by Joseph A. Weingarten. New York, New York: 330 Cherry Street. Vols. 1-2, No. 2. May 1943–June/July 1944. Irregular (monthly and bimonthly). [Eleven issues.] CtY (incomplete), MdBJ, NN

1944

88. *Contact Book.* A Trade Directory of Film, Stage, Radio, Agent, Hotel, Producer, Newspaper, Night Club, Publishing Contacts in New York City. New York, New York: Celebrity Service, Inc. 1944. [*Standard Periodical Directory*, p. 305, dates first issue as 1939.] NN

489. *Curtain Call.* A Monthly Magazine. Published in the Interest of Show Folks of America and Everywhere. Edited by Dorothee Bates. Chicago, Illinois: 1839 West Monroe Street. [Nos. 1-2.] April–May 1944. Monthly. [Mimeographed. April 1944 issue called a sample copy.] MH

490. *Players Guide.* A Pictorial Directory for the Legitimate Theatre. Edited by Terese Hayden (1944-1945); with P. L. Ross (1946–). New York, New York: 205 West 54th Street. August 1944–1945. Semiannual. 1946–. Annual. [Published by Actors' Equity Association, Fall 1945–1950. Sponsored by the Actors' Equity Association, 1951– (with the Chorus Equity Association, 1951–1955; the American Federation of Radio Artists, 1951–1952; and the American Federation of Television and Radio Artists, 1953–). The subtitle varies slightly.] DLC, NN

491. *Stage Pictorial.* New York, New York. Vols. 1-3, No. 5. [Spring 1944]–July 1946. Irregular. [Vol. 1 complete in one issue.] DLC (2-3), MH ([1]-[3]), NN, NhD ([1-3]), PP

492. *The Theatrical Calendar.* Current and Future Activities in the New York Theatre. New York, New York: Published by Celebrity Service, Inc., 150 East 54th Street. 23 April 1944–26 December 1948. Weekly. [Mimeographed.] NN (incomplete; forty-seven issues)

493. *University of Washington Publications in Drama.* Edited by Glenn Hughes. Seattle, Washington: University of Washington Press. Vols. 1-2. 1944–1945. Annual. IaU, ICU, WU

1945

494. *The New Conjurors' Magazine.* Edited by W. B. Gibson. New York, New York: Conjurors' Press, Inc., 148 Lafayette Street. Vol. 1, No. 1. February 1945. Then, *The Conjurors' Magazine.* Vol. 1, No. 2–Vol. 5, No. 7. March 1945–September 1949. Monthly (no issue for February 1946). [Official Organ of the Magician's Guild. Founded as a revival of the *Conjurors' Monthly Magazine*, 1906–1908. Absorbed by *Genii.*] DLC (missing Vol. 3), MH, NN

495. *Notes on the American Theatre.* Issued Periodically for Soviet Theatre Artists by the Theatre Committee, National Council of American Soviet Friendship. New York, New York: 114 East 32nd Street. Vol. 1, Nos. 1-3. August 1945–January 1946. Irregular. [Mimeographed.] NN (Nos. 1-2 are photostat reproductions; No. 3 is mutilated.)

496. *Prologue. The Tufts College Theater.* Medford, Massachusetts: Tufts College Theater. Vols. 1–10. December 1945–1955. Then, *Prologue. The Tufts University Theater.* Vol. 11–. 1955–. Irregular (three to four issues a year). [I have not been able to locate any issue prior to Vol. 9, No. 1, November 1953.] MMeT (Vol. 9–), NN (Vol. 9–)

97. *Theatre World.* Edited by Daniel Blum (1944/45–1963/64); John Willis (1964/65–). New York, New York: Crown Publishers, Inc. 1944/45–. Annual. [Title varies.] CtY, MH, MiU, NN, OU

1946 (See also *Magic Is Fun,* Addenda, p. 87.)

98. *American Repertory Theatre.* News of the Theatre in American Life. Executive Director, Inez Simons. Hollywood, California: American Repertory Theatre, Post Office Box 886. Vol. 1, Nos. 1-9. August 1946–April 1947. Monthly. [The subtitle varies.] C, NN

99. *Bandwagon.* Camden, Ohio; Richmond, Indiana. February 1946–December 1953; [Series 2], January 1954–[May?] 1957; [Series 3], [June?] 1957–. [August–December 1951 not published. Organ of the Burnt Corkers, January–November 1947; February 1946–July 1947 as *Hobby-Swapper*; August 1947–July 1951, *Hobby Bandwagon*; August 1951–June 1960, *C.H.S. Bandwagon*. Absorbed *Bandwagon* (Circus Historical Society) in July 1947.] NN

00. *Footlights.* A Stage Magazine Devoted to the Community and Little Theatres of America. Edited by Frederick Barnes. Milwaukee, Wisconsin: American Theatre Association, Inc., Plankington Bldg., 161 N. Wisconsin Ave. Vol. 1, No. 1. July 1946. Monthly. CSt, DLC, MH, NNC, ViU, ViW, VRU

01. *Hobby-Swapper.* A Monthly Magazine Devoted to Hobby Trading. Camden, Ohio: Harry M. Simpson, Publisher, 122 S. Main Street. Vol. 1, No. 1. February 1946. Then, Vol. 1, No. 2–Vol. 2, No. 6. [Subtitle changes.] Then, *Hobby Bandwagon.* Vol. 2, No. 7–Vol. 6, No. 6. August 1947–July 1951. Then, *C.H.S. Bandwagon.* Vol. 7, No. 1. January 1951. Monthly. NN

02. *Little Theatre Guide.* A Magazine Devoted to the Little Theatres of America. Edited by Jack Ferdie. Chicago, Illinois: Published by Little Theatre Guide, 624 S. Michigan Ave. Vol. 1, No. 2. April 1946. Monthly. [This is the only issue I have been able to locate.] MH

03. *Notes on the Soviet Theatre.* Issued Periodically by the Theatre Committee, National Council of American Soviet Friendship. New York, New York, 114 East 32nd Street. Vol. 1, No. 1. February 1946. Irregular. Mimeographed. [The copy at the New York Public Library is rapidly disintegrating. Also known as *The Soviet Theatre.*] NN

04. *Pacific Theatre.* A Monthly Publication. Edited by Arthur Koenig. Santa Monica, California: A. Koenig, 1655 Euclid Street. Vols. 1-2, No. 6. 1946–November 1947. Monthly (irregular). [I have not been able to discover any issues of Vol. 1.] DLC ([2]), NN ([2])

05. *The Shakespeare Society of New Orleans.* Publications for the year 1946. Edited by Edward Alexander Parsons. New Orleans, Louisiana: Pub-

lished by the Society, 1946. [Contains three poems, and an essay by Wolfgang J. Weilgart on *Macbeth*.] NN

506. *Talent Review*. Stage. Screen. Radio. Music. Dance. Incorporating *Hollywood Herald Magazine*. Activities of the Experimental and Legitimate Theatre. Hollywood, California. Vol. 1, No. 8–Vol. 6, No. 2. 2 November 1946–12 February 1949. Monthly (to September 1946); biweekly. [I have not been able to locate any copies of Vol. 1, Nos. 1-7. The subtitle varies. Vol. 2, No. 1 (4 January 1947) numbered Vol. 2, No. 11. The microfilm copy at the New York Public Library contains only eighteen issues.] NN ([1–6] and on microfilm; incomplete), CSt ([1]-[8]), NNC ([1-4])

1947

507. *Chicago Stagebill Yearbook, 1947*. A Pictorial and Statistical Review of the Theatrical Season of 1946-47, with a Chronological History of the 24 Preceding Years on the Chicago Stage. Edited by William Leonard. Chicago, Illinois: Published by Chicago Stagebill, Fieberg Press. 1947. Annual. [The editor says that he wants it to be an annual.] DLC, IC, ICU, NN

508. *Curtain Call*. Edited by Alice G. Owen. Dover, New Jersey: Published by the Dover Little Theatre. Vol. 13, No. 11–Vol. 23, No. 2. September 1947–December 1956. Monthly. [News Bulletin of the Dover Little Theatre. I have not been able to locate the earlier volumes.] NN (film)

509. *Detroit Stage Call Board*. Edited by Ross J. Chepeleff. Detroit, Michigan: Detroit Stage. Vols. 1-2, No. 1. [Five issues.] 8 July–6 October 1947. Irregular [when program changed]. MiD

510. *Prologue and Epilogue*. St. Louis, Missouri: Published by the St. Louis Resident Theatre. Vol. 1, No. 1. February 1947. Monthly. Then, *Prologue*. Vol. 1, No. 2–Vol. 2, [No. 11]. March 1947–November 1948. [Includes an unnumbered special supplement, dated August 1948. Vol. 2, Nos. 9-11, are called Nos. 19-21.] MoS, NN

511. *The Prompt Box*. American Theatre Wing Professional and Technical Training Program. War Service, Inc. Edited by Guy Biondi. New York, New York: ATW, 730 Fifth Avenue. Vols. 1-9, No. 5. 15 March 1947–10 August 1953. Irregular. [Fifty-seven issues. Vols. 3-9, No. 5 (October 1947–10 August 1953) have the title superimposed on the initials "ATW."] CSt ([1-8]), NN (missing Vol. 9, No. 5?)

512. *Scene*. Dallas, Texas: 305 Melba Building. Vol. 1. 1947. Monthly. [*Bulletin of the New York Public Library*, LI (June 1947), 400. In answer to my letter, Mr. Mark A. Altermann, theatre librarian at Dallas Public Library, writes that the library has no copies. All he was able to learn "from someone's memory" was that "the periodical lived only a few months and folded."]

13. *Theatre Craft.* Edited by A. C. Sanucci. Glendale, California: Published by A. C. Sanucci, 1513 Randal Street. Vols. 1-2, No. 5. January 1947–May 1948. Monthly. [Seventeen issues.] DLC

14. *The Wisconsin Idea Theatre.* Edited by Junius Eddy (May 1947–June 1949); Ronald C. Gee (September 1949–Fall 1952); Gerald Kahan (Winter 1952/53–Summer 1953); Ronald C. Gee (Fall 1953–Winter 1953/54.) Madison, Wisconsin: The University of Wisconsin. Vols. 1-7, No. 4. May 1947–Winter 1953/54. Then, *Wisconsin Stage.* Vols. 8-10, No. 2. Spring 1954–Summer 1956. Quarterly. [Mimeographed.] NN (missing Vol. 9, No. 2), WU, WaU

1948

15. *Chrysalis.* The Pocket Revue of the Arts. Edited by Lily and Baird Hastings. Boston, Massachusetts. Vols. 1-14, No. 12. 1948–1961. Bimonthly. NN (Vol. 2, No. 1–Vol. 4, No. 12), NmU (missing Vol. 1), RPB

16. *Footnotes.* Charleston's Oldest Community Theatre. Charleston, South Carolina: Footlight Players, Inc., Dock St. Theatre, 135 Church Street. Vols. 1-16, No. 2. September 1948–1963. Then, *Footlights.* From the Footlight Players, Inc. in the Dock Street Theatre. Vol. 16, No. 3–. January 1964–. Irregular (to six issues a year). DLC, NN

17. *Poetry Book Magazine.* (Waldorf Book Club). Brooklyn, New York. Vols. 1-7. Fall 1948–Summer 1955. Quarterly. Then, *Poetry and Drama Magazine.* City Island, New York. Vol. 8, No. 1–. 1956–. Biannual. CoDU, MH ([1]), MdBE, NBuU, NN

18. *Show of the Month News.* New York, New York: Show of the Month Club, 1050 Sixth Avenue. Vol. 1, No. 3; Vol. 2, No. 1. Summer 1948; November 1948. [I have been unable to locate any other issues.] NN

19. *The Swan of Avon.* A Quarterly Dealing with New Shakespearean Research. Edited by Rudolf Melander. Santa Barbara, California: Published and Distributed by the Melander Shakespeare Society (R. Melander, Founder). Vol. 1, Nos. 1-3. 30 March–30 September 1948. Quarterly. [All the articles seem to be by Melander.] CL, CU, CtY, DFo, FU, MH, MiU, NN, NcU, OCU, PP, TxU

20. *Theatre Business Review.* A Service Exclusively for T. O. A. Members. [Theatre Owners of America.] New York, New York: 1501 Broadway. No. 1. February 1948. [The entire issue is devoted to television. There is no indication of what future issues were to contain.] NN

21. *Theatre Quarterly.* A Publication Devoted to Community Theatre. Edited by Ira Jacob Bilowit. New York, New York: Published by Ira Jacob Bilowit for the City College Theatre Workshop, College of the City of New York. Vol. 1, No. 1. November 1948. Quarterly. [Free.] NN

1949

522. *Broadway Sign Post.* A Monthly Review of Current Plays and Motion Pictures. Edited by Margaret Wentworth. New York, New York: Published by D. F. Mendola, 236 West 55th Street. Vols. 1-3, No. 7. [Twenty-three issues.] 5 February 1949–May 1952. Monthly. [Mimeographed. Publication suspended June 1950–October 1951. Successor to Margaret Wentworth's *Sign Post.*] CSt, DLC, MdBG, MH, NN, NPV, NjT

523. *Bulletin of the Comediantes.* Published by The Comediantes, An Informal International Group of All Those Interested in the "Comedia." Edited by Everett W. Hesse; later by Karl-Ludwig Selig; then by Warren T. McCready (January 1967–). Madison, Wisconsin: University of Wisconsin, Department of Speech and Drama. [Printed privately in the city chosen by the business manager. In 1967, in Tucson, Arizona, the University of Arizona.] Spring 1949–. Semi-annual. [Mimeographed until Spring 1951, when it began to be printed.] NN (Vol. 4, No. 2–), WU, WaU, WvU

524. *Curtain Going Up.* Edited by William Talbot. New York, New York: Samuel French, Inc., 25 W. 45th Street. [Vol. 1.] Inaugural edition. November 1949. DLC

525. *Educational Theatre Journal.* Edited variously by Barnard Hewitt, Darkes Albright, Hubert Heffner, James Clancy, O. G. Brockett, Jonathan Curvin, and Francis Hodge. Washington, D.C.: American Educational Theatre Association, John F. Kennedy Center, 1701 Pennsylvania Ave., N.W. Vol. 1–. 1949–. Quarterly. CU, DLC, ICL, MiU NN, NjP, OClW, WaU

526. *Puppetry Journal.* Edited by George Latshaw, and later, by Vivian Michael. Asheville, Ohio: Published by the Puppeteers of America. Vols. 1-15, No. 6. 1949–May/June, 1964. Bimonthly. [The issues in Vol. 1 are not dated. Superseded the *Grapevine Telegraph of the Puppeteers of America.*] NN

527. *Theatre, Arena & Auditorium Guide, 1949.* Edited and Compiled by Hal Oliver. New York, New York: Published by the Association of Theatrical Press Agents and Managers, 25 West 45th Street. 1949. Annual. DLC, NN

528. *Theatre Time Magazine.* Edited by William Keegan. New York, New York: By Theatre Publications, Inc., 152 West 42nd Street. Vols. 1-3, No. 4. [Ten issues.] Spring 1949–Winter 1952. Quarterly (irregular, as three issues a year). [The index is in Vol. 3, No. 4.] CaB, CL, CoU, DLC, KyU, NN, OU, PP, PU

1950

29. *The AGVA News.* Edited by Alvin Brandt. New York, New York: American Guild of Variety Artists, 110 West 57th Street [later, 551 Fifth Avenue]. Vol. 1–. 1950–. Irregular (August 1950–August 1952); Monthly (irregular to nine times a year, July 1953–.) DLC (6–), NIC ([3]–), NN (1-[2-3])

30. *ANTA News.* New York, New York: American National Theatre and Academy. March 1950–December 1952; April–June 1953. [Publication was suspended, July 1950–1951, July 1953–February 1955.] Irregular. [Superseded by *ANTA Newsletter.*] NN

31. *Dancing Star.* San Jose, California. Vols. 1-7. 1950–1957. Then, *Dance Digest.* Vols. 8-12, No. 2. 1957–March/April 1962. Irregular. CoD ([1]–), CSf (1-[11]), DLC ([1]–)

32. *Folk Dance Federation of Washington.* Seattle, Washington. October 1950–November 1954. Then, *Footnotes.* 1954–. Irregular. FU (1-[3]), NN

33. *Magicol.* Magic, Juggling, Ventriloquism, etc. Official Bulletin of the Magic Collectors Association. Edited by Morris N. Young, M. D. New York, New York: 170 Broadway. Vols. 1-3, No. 1. [Nine issues.] August 1950–August/September 1952. Quarterly. NN

34. *Shakespeare Quarterly.* Edited by James G. McManaway. New York, New York: 322 E. 57th Street [later, Washington, D.C., 201 East Capitol Street]. Vol. 1, No. 1–. January 1950–. [Succeeds *Shakespeare Association of America Bulletin.*] CLU, CtY, DLC, ICN, IEN, IU, IaU, KU, LU, MH, MiD, MiU, MoS, NN, NjP, OCU, OU, PU, TU, ViU, WaU

35. *Stanford Players Newsletter.* Stanford, California: Published by the Stanford Players of Stanford University, Department of Speech and Drama. Nos. 1-7. Winter 1950–Spring 1953. Irregular. CL ([1950–1952]), NN

36. *Summer Theatres.* Actors Cues. New York, New York: Leo Shull Publications, 155 West 46th Street. 1950–. Annual. DLC (incomplete), WM (incomplete)

37. *Theatre News Weekly.* A Publication Devoted to the Best Interests of Patron, Artist, Playwright, Executive, Ticket Agent and All Who Are a Part of the Legitimate Theatre Industry. Edited by Mercer W. Sweeney. New York, New York: Owned and Published Weekly by Staff Associates, Inc., 373 West 52nd Street. Vols. 1-3, Nos. 1-43. [14 April?] 1950–2 February 1951. Weekly. [The issue for 2 February 1951 says that the paper will discontinue with the issue of 9 February.] NN (missing Nos. 1-5, 14, 16-17, 19-20, 22-36)

1951

538. *AETA Directory.* American Educational Theatre Association. East Lansing, Michigan. 1951–1961/62; Evanston, Illinois: Northwestern University. 1962/63–1964/65; Washington, D.C.: John F. Kennedy Center for the Performing Arts. 1965/66–. [Vol. 1–]. 1951–. Annual. C (1951–1953, 1955, 1959/60–), C-S (1959/60–), NIC (1962/63–), OkS (1951–)

539. *Critical Digest.* The Weekly NYC Theatre Newsletter Digest Service for College, Resident and Community Theatres and Libraries. Edited by Ted Kraus. New York, New York: Ted Kraus, GPO Box 2403. Vol. 1, No. 1–. September 1951–. Weekly (biweekly in June, July, August). NN (June 1954–.)

540. *International Theatre.* Edited by Wolf Heider. New York, New York: I. T. Magazine, Inc., 17 East 45th Street. Spring 1951. [Preview edition.] Vol. 1, No. 1. January–February 1955. Bimonthly. CoU, InU, MH, NN, NjP, PU

541. *Plays and Players.* Edited by Frederick O. Schubert. Chicago, Illinois: Schubert Publications, Inc., 220 S. Michigan Avenue. Vol. 1, Nos. 1-2. October–November 1951. Monthly. [A play in each issue.] CL, DLC ([1]–), NN

542. *The Prompter.* Cambridge, Massachusetts: Published by a Committee of the Brattle Theatre Associates in Cooperation with Members of the Brattle Theatre. Vol. 1, No. 1. Spring, January 1951. DLC

543. *Ring Theatre Annual.* Coral Gables, Florida: University of Miami. 1951/52. Annual. NN

544. *The Shakespeare Newsletter.* Edited by Louis Marder. New York, New York: 749 Franklin D. Roosevelt Drive [later, Chicago, Illinois: University of Chicago, Chicago Circle Campus]. Vol. 1, No. 1–. March 1951–. Monthly (except July and August). CtY, DLC, ICN, ICU, LU, MB, MH, NIC, NN, NNC, OClW, PU, TU, WaU

545. *Shaw Society of America Bulletin.* University Park, Pennsylvania: Sparks Building. Vol. 1, Nos. 1-2. February–Autumn 1951. Then, *Shaw Bulletin.* Vol. 1, No. 3–Vol. 2, No. 6. [1952]–September 1958. Then, *The Shaw Review.* Vol. 2, No. 7–January 1959–. Irregular (1951–1956); three numbers a year (1957–). [The numbering is irregular.] CL, CLSU, CtY, IEN, IU, LU, MH, MiU, NIC, NNC, PU, TxU, WU

546. *Southwest Theatre Conference Bulletin.* Fort Worth, Texas: Texas Christian University. Vol. 1, Nos. 1-3. 25/27 October 1951–September 1952. Irregular. NN

547. *Who's Where.* Tells Who's Where in Show Business. Edited by Allen Zwerdling (until 1956), and by Claire Shull (until 1960). New York, New York: Show Business, 136 West 44th Street. 1951–1961. Annual. [Was *Actors Cues Directory,* published 1941–1951. There seems to be no issue in 1952.] CL, NN

1952

48. *Curtain Time.* Edited by Thomas Stasink. New York, New York: Fireside Theatre, 277 Park Avenue. 1952–. Irregular. NN

49. *Pasadena Playhouse Curtain Call.* Pasadena, California: Pasadena Playhouse, 39 S. El Molina. Vol. 3, No. 3–[Vol. 13, No. 4]. December 1952–June 1963. Very irregular. [Volume and numbering of issues dropped after Vol. 8, No. 17, January 1959. It was not published in April, August, and October 1957 and in April, June, August, and October 1958.] CLSU ([4]–)

1953

50. *Greek Theatre Magazine.* Official Publication of the Most Beautiful Outdoor Theatre in the World. Edited by Douglas Crane and Mary L. Lacy (1953–1960); Mary L. Lacy (1961); Alyce Wiley (1962–1965); Barbara Huber (1965–1967). Hollywood, California: Playgoer Publications, Inc., 1149 N. McCadden Place. 6 July 1953–. [Published for each theater production during the season, June through September.] NN

51. *Theatre.* Edited by John Chapman. New York, New York: Random House. [Vols. 1-4.] 1953–1956. Annual. CL, DLC, ICN, IEN, MiU, NB, NIC, NN, NjP, NjR, OCU, OU, PSt, WU

1954

52. *The Actors Magazine.* Edited by Lyle Kenyon Engel. New York, New York: Published by The Actors Magazine, Inc., 1 East 42nd Street. Vol. 1, No. 1. February/March 1954. Bimonthly. [Has a play, *Point Blank*, by Ben Rodin.] NN

53. *Center.* A Magazine of the Performing Arts. Edited by Robert Hatch. New York, New York: The City Center of Music and Drama, Inc., 130 West 56th Street. Vols. 1-3, No. 1. February 1954–April 1956. Irregular. [Fourteen issues. Although the magazine was to be published ten times a year it was published seven times in 1954, six times in 1955, and once in 1956.] CL, CLU, CU, DLC, GU, IU, MH, MiU (Vols. 1-2), MoS, NN, OU, TxDA

54. *Central Opera Service Bulletin.* New York, New York: Central Opera Service, 147 W. 39th Street. 1954–. Irregular. [The 1954 date is given in the *Standard Periodical Directory*, p. 634.] CU ([1960]–), DLC ([1963]–), NN (1959–)

55. *Chapter One.* New York, New York: Published by Greater New York Chapter of ANTA, 1545 Broadway [later, 245 West 52nd Street]. Vols. 1-12, No. 1. January 1954–Winter 1965. Monthly (during the theater

season, with some irregularities). Irregular (with Vol. 6). ICU (incomplete), IU (incomplete), NN (incomplete)

556. *Educational Theatre News.* Official Publication of the American Educational Theatre Association, Southern California Section. Long Beach, California. Los Angeles, California: Published by the Southern California Section, American Educational Theatre Association, University of California at Los Angeles, Royce Hall, 229. Vol. 1–. 1 February 1954–. Monthly (1 February–April 1954); Six issues a year (Vol. 2, No. 1–). October 1954–. [Various editors. The place of publication changes.] CL, NN

557. *Lyric Opera Program.* Edited by Al Berman. Chicago, Illinois: Lyric Opera Program Division, Midwest Publishing Co., Inc. 740 N. Rush Street. 1954–. Five times (during the opera season, 7 October–15 December). [*Standard Periodical Directory,* p. 636.]

558. *Negro Theatre Spotlight.* New York, New York: S. Green & C. S. Griffin. No. 1. July 1954. [Affiliated with Acme Theatre.] CtY, DLC

559. *The OSU Theatre Collection Bulletin.* A Publication Devoted to Research in Theatre History Conducted in the Ohio State University Theatre Collection. Columbus, Ohio: Ohio State University. [No. 1]–. Autumn 1954–. Irregular [from one to two issues a year]. CLU, CtY, DLC, GU, IEN, IU, InU, KyU, MiU, MnU, MoU, NBu, NNC, OU, RU

560. *Opera Annual.* American Edition. New York, New York. 1954/55–. Annual. AzU, CLU, LU, MoS (1955/56–)

561. *Stage and Arena News.* For Producers Only. Edited by Robert Garland. New York, New York: Stage and Arena Guild, 140 West 55th Street. Vol. 2, No. 2. Indian Summer 1954. [I have not been able to discover any earlier issues. Mimeographed.] NN [2]

562. *Stubs.* The Seating Plan Guide for New York Theatres, Music Halls and Sports Stadia with Partial Coverage of Other Cities. New York, New York: L. Tobin. [Vols. 1–6.] 1954–1960. Annual. [A second edition was published in 1958. There is no issue for 1959.] NN

563. *Theatre Arts News Service.* A News Service for Entertainment Editors, Compiled by the Editors of Theatre Arts. New York, New York: Published by National Theatre Arts Council, 130 W. 56th Street. Vol. 1, No. 8–Vol. 3, No. 12. October 1954–December 1956. Monthly. [A Broadside. I have not been able to locate the first seven issues.] NN (missing Vol. 1, Nos. 1-7)

564. *Theatre Scoop Sheets.* New York, New York. Nos. 1-29. [April?–October?] 1954. Irregular. [The title is supplied from the publisher's envelope. Issued in looseleaf format.] NN (missing Nos. 1-13)

565. *Yale Drama Alumni Newsletter.* Yale Drama Alumni Association. New Haven, Connecticut: Yale University, School of Drama. [Nos. 1-6, i.e., 8.] 24 December 1954–1960. Irregular. CtY

1955

66. *ANTA Newsletter.* Edited by George Freedley (Nos. 1-2, March–May 1955); Ruth M. Mayleas (Nos. 3-30, September 1955–April 1963). New York, New York: The American National Theatre and Academy, 139 West 44th Street. Nos. 1-30. March 1955–April 1963. Irregular (three to four issues a year). [Absorbed *ANTA Spotlight*, February 1963. Superseded by *ANTA News Bulletin.*] IU, LU (missing No. 1), MiD, NN

67. *The Carleton Drama Review.* Northfield, Minnesota: Published by the Carleton Players, Carleton College. Vol. 1, Nos. 1-2. Fall 1955–1956. Then, *Tulane Drama Review.* New Orleans, Louisiana: Tulane University, Department of Theatre and Speech. Vol. 1, No. 3–Vol. 11. January 1957-Summer 1967. Then, *The Drama Review.* New York, New York: New York University. Vol. 12, No. 1–. Fall 1967–. CL, CoU, FMU, IU, IaU, KU, LU, MiU, NIC, NN, NNU, OCU, PU, RPB, TxU

68. *Community Theatre Bulletin.* New York State Community Theatre Association and Extension Service of New York State College of Agriculture. Ithaca, New York: Published by New York State College of Agriculture. Department of Rural Sociology. At Cornell University. March 1955–September 1960. Quarterly. [Mimeographed. With December 1960 the title changes to *New York State Community Theatre Journal.*] DLC ([1955-1959]-1960), NN (missing all before 1959)

69. *Harlequin.* Edited by Barbara Fry and W. R. Lasater (1957); by Barbara Fry (1959). [Vol. 1]–Vol. 3, No. 1. [There is question whether Vol. 1, 1955, was published.] Los Angeles, California: P. O. Box 75-451, Sanford Station. Vol. 2, No. 1. 1957. Hermosa Beach, California: P. O. Box 296. Vol. 3, No. 1. 1959. Irregular. [No information regarding frequency.] CU ([3]), IU, RPB, NN

70. *The Little Theatre Bulletin.* Boston, Massachusetts. Vol. 1, No. 1. September 1955. NN

71. *NJTL Bulletin.* Chatham, New Jersey: Published by the New Jersey Theatre League, 117 Western Avenue. Vols. 7-12, No. 4. November 1955–January 1961. Then, *New Jersey Theatre League Bulletin.* Vol. 12, No. 5–. March 1961–. Monthly (irregular). [Mimeographed. I have not been able to locate the issues before Vol. 7, November 1955. Seemingly it was established in 1949.] NN (Vol. 8, 1956+), NjP (12+), NjPSC ([5-15]+)

72. *Playhouse Reporter.* Nashville, Tennessee: Nashville Community Playhouse, 2102 Belcourt Ave. Vols. 1-4. No. 6. October 1955–May 1958. [Nos. 1-18.] Monthly (during Community Playhouse season). [Some twelve different editors are listed during the brief history of the magazine.] T (missing Vol. 1, No. 3)

573. *Pocket Celebrity Scrapbook.* New York, New York: Pocket Magazines, Inc., 1140 Broadway. Vol. 1. 1955. DLC

574. *Simon's Directory of Theatrical Materials Services and Information.* New York, New York: Bernard Simon, 1674 Broadway. Vol. 1. 1955–. Annual. CL, CLSU, DLC, MB, NN, NNC

1956

575. *Actors Forum.* Published by the Actors Forum Guild. Edited by Emmett Groseclose. New York, New York: Box 164, Planetarium Station. Vol. 1, Nos. 1-4. November 1956–February 1957. Monthly. [Mimeographed.] NN

576. *The Alice Gerstenberg Experimental Theatre Workshop.* [Founded 4 December 1955 by Paul Edward Pross and Otto E. Anderson.] Chicago, Illinois: Alice Gerstenberg Experimental Theatre Workshop, Studio 212, 840 Argyle. [Nos. 1-2.] 1956/57–1957/58. NN

577. *The American National Theatre and Academy: Minutes of the Annual Membership Meeting of the American National Theatre and Academy.* New York, New York: 1545 Broadway. [Vols. 1-7.] 1956–1963. Annual. [Mimeographed.] InU (1958–1963), NN (1958–1963)

578. *The Catholic Preview of Entertainment.* Edited by Stephen L. Saunders. Carmel, New York. Vols. 1-2, No. 8. [Twenty issues.] November 1956–June 1958. Monthly. CSt, DLC, PPiD

579. *Curtain Call Magazine.* Edited by George S. McGregor. Harlingen, Texas. Vol. 1, No. 1. June 1956. Monthly. [Devoted to the Little Theatre.] DLC, MoS (not there)

580. *International Theatre Annual.* Edited by H. Hobson. New York, New York: Citadel Press. [Nos. 1-4.] 1956–1959. Annual. MiU, NN (1956, 1957, 1959), OU

581. *Lyric Opera News.* Official Publication of the Lyric Opera of Chicago. Chicago, Illinois: Lyric Opera of Chicago, 20 N. Wacker Drive. 1956–. Three times a year (irregular). IU ([2]–), NN ([3]–), WM (3–)

582. *NOA Newsletter.* Evanston, Illinois: Northwestern University, National Opera Association, c/o Robert Gay, Director of Opera at Northwestern. 1956–. Five times a year. [*Standard Periodical Directory*, p. 637.]

583. *Performing Arts.* Edited by Mervin Leeds. Published by Agreement between the Performing Arts Committee, the San Francisco Dance League, and the Editor. San Francisco, California: 2127 Broderick Street. Nos. 1-21. December 1956–August/September 1961. Bimonthly. ["Covers activities in dance, drama, & music by resident-artists . . . in 13 Western States."] FU, NN (Nos. 1-19)

584. *Shaw Society Newsletter.* Chicago, Illinois: Shaw Society of Chicago. October 1956–. Irregular. DLC

585. *Southern Theatre News.* A Quarterly News Magazine. Edited by James

Byrd. [Edited also by Arthur McDonald.] Salisbury, North Carolina: Published by the South Eastern Theatre Conference, Central Office, Catawba College. Vol. 1, No. 2. Fall 1956. Then, *Southern Theatre News*. A Seasonal News Magazine. Vol. 1, No. 2–Vol. 6, No. 4. Winter 1957–Summer 1962. Then, *Southern Theatre*. Vols. 7-8, No. 2. Fall 1962–Summer 1964. Quarterly. [Place of publication moved to St. Andrews College, Laurinburg, North Carolina. The periodical more or less covers ten states.] FMU ([5]–), GU (6–), NN ([1-2]-[6]–)

1957

86. *AETA Projects Progress Newsletter*. American Educational Theatre Association. Minneapolis, Minnesota. Vol. 1. 1957. [I have not been able to obtain any further details.] ICA (not retained), OU (not retained)

87. *ASTR Newsletter*. Edited by Gerald E. Bentley (April 1957–October 1960); Marguerite McAveny (April 1961–). New York, New York: Published by the American Society for Theatre Research. April 1957–. Approximately two issues a year (irregular). [Eighteen issues by Summer 1967.] NN, NjP

88. *American National Theatre and Academy: National Theatre Service. Service Pamphlet*. New York, New York. June 1957. [I have not been able to locate any other issues. Whether this should be considered a serial is questionable.] NN

89. *Broadway's Best*. The Complete Record of the Theatrical Year. Edited by John Chapman. Garden City, New York: Doubleday & Company, Inc., 277 Park Avenue. [Vols. 1-4.] 1957–1960. Annual. CLU, DeU, DLC, GEU, IU, MB, MH, MiU, NIC, NNC, TxU

90. *Catholic Theatre '57*. National Catholic Theatre Conference Annual. Edited by Edgar L. Kloten. Dubuque, Iowa. Printed. 1957. Annual. NN

91. *Funspot*. The Magazine of Amusement Management. Cincinnati, Ohio: Billboard Publishing Co., 2160 Patterson Street. Vols. 1-4, No. 12. August 1957–December 1960. [Merged with the *Outdoor-Show News* section of *Billboard Music Week* to form *Amusement Business*. Vol. 73. 1961.] DLC, IU, MoS (2–), OU (2–)

92. *Guide to the Performing Arts*. New York, New York: The Scarecrow Press. 1957–. Annual. CSt, CU, CoU, DLC, IEN, IU, IaU, LNHT, MiD, MH, NN, OCl, WU

93. *Playbill*. A Weekly Magazine for Theatregoers. New York, New York. Vol. 1–. September 1957–. Weekly. [Programs of plays given in New York City.] CU ([3]–), IaU (1–), NjP (8–)

94. *Straw Hat*. Guide to Summer Theatres, Musical Tents, Shakespeare Festivals. New York, New York. 1957. Annual. DLC, MB, MoU, NN, NNC, WU

1958

595. *ANTA-LA Newsletter.* Greater Los Angeles Chapter. American National Theatre and Academy. Hollywood, California: 2301 N. Highland. 1958–. Quarterly (irregular). [When the title changed to *ANTA Newsletter*, the magazine changed the city of publication to Los Angeles, 6423 Wilshire Boulevard.] CLU

596. *The ANTA Spotlight.* A Backstage Bulletin for Group Members of the American Theatre and Academy. Edited by Ruth M. Mayleas (Nos. 1-7, October 1958–July 1960). [Drops the name of the editor. Later edited by Shirley Wilbur.] New York, New York: 1545 Broadway. [Vols. 1-2], Nos. 1-16. October 1958–October 1962. Quarterly (irregular). [Mimeographed. Absorbed by *ANTA Newsletter*.] CLU, IU, LU, MiD, NN, PPiU

597. *Chorus.* Boulder, Colorado: University of Colorado Theatre. Nos. 1–. March 1958–. Irregular. CoU

598. *Critique.* A Critical Review of Theatre Arts and Literature. Edited variously by Robert Smett, Sr. Mary Marguerite, and Hugh Dickinson. Buffalo, New York: Published by the National Theatre Conference. Vol. 1, Nos. 1-2. February–May 1958. Then, *Drama Critique.* A Critical Review of Theatre Arts and Literature. Detroit, Michigan: Published three times yearly by the National Catholic Theatre Conference. Vol. 1, No. 3–Vol. 11, No. 3. December 1958–Fall, 1968. Three issues a year. ArU, CLU, GU, ICL, IU, MiD, MH, NIC, NjP, NN, TxU

599. *Drama Studies.* Prepared by Joseph Mersand. General editor, William Lewin. Summit, New Jersey: Copyright by Educational & Recreational Guides, Inc., 10 Brainerd Road. Vol. 1, No. 1. February 1958. DLC

600. *The Harlequin.* Edited by John A. Mang, Jr. Charlottesville, Virginia: Harlequin Magazine Corporation, Box 3343 University Station. Vols. 1-2, [Nos. 1-6]. November 1958–Christmas 1959. Quarterly. [A student enterprise independent of the university.] ViU

601. *Modern Drama.* Lawrence, Kansas: Department of English, University of Kansas. Vol. 1–. 1958–. Quarterly. CLU, DLC, FU, GU, ICL, IEN, IU, IaU, KU, KyU, MH, MiU, NIC, NN, NNC, NjP, OU, PU, WU, WaU

602. *On Stage.* Edited by Alice Spivak. New York, New York: Courtesy of Eaves Costume Company, 151 West 46th Street. Vol. 1, Nos. 1-7. October 1958–May 1959. Monthly. [Not published in February 1959. *New Serial Titles*, II (1964), 1742, says: "Suspended between May, 1959, and Spring, 1963."] CaAEU, NN

603. *The Prompter.* Edited by Earl Schuller (August–October 1958); Ray Fisher (November–December 1958). Los Angeles, California: Prompter Publications, 10634 W. Pico Boulevard. Vol. 1, Nos. 1-5. August–

December 1958. [Preceded by a preliminary number dated June? 1958.] Monthly. CLU

1959

604. *Americada*. Magazine of the American Academy of Dramatic Arts. Edited by William Como. New York, New York: Published by the American Academy of Dramatic Arts, 245 West 52nd Street. Vol. 1, No. 1. Spring, 1959. Quarterly. NN

605. *Ballet Aficionados*. Newsletter. New Brunswick, New Jersey: 271½ Somerset Street. No. 1. 1959. [I have not been able to discover any other information concerning this magazine.] DLC (not retained)

606. *Children's Theatre Conference Newsletter*. Edited by Werdna Finley. [Vols. 9-11.] Olympia, Washington: Published Quarterly by The Children's Theatre Press, The Coach House Press, Inc., and Samuel French, Inc. Vol. 9, No. 2-Vol. 11, No. 3. April 1959-May 1962. Quarterly. [No. 4 is numbered 3. Supposedly begun in 1951. I have not been able to locate any copies earlier than those listed here.] NN (9-11)

607. *Children's Theatre Research*. Edited and Published by Oriel J. Willert. Glendora, California, P. O. Box 41. [With Vol. 1, No. 9, it moves to the Department of Speech, the University of Utah, Salt Lake City, Utah.] Vol. 1, Nos. 1-10. April 1959-March 1960. Monthly (except July and August). CLSU, GU, NN (missing Nos. 4, 5, 8)

608. *Dance Perspectives*. Brooklyn, New York. No. 1-. Winter 1959-. CL, CaOTU, DLC, ICU, InU, MdU, N, NcGW, NIC, NNC, NbU, TxU, WU

609. *Experiment Theatre Anthology*. Edited by Carol Ely Harper. Seattle, Washington: Experiment Press, 6565 Windermere Road. [Vol. 1.] 1959. [There is no indication that another issue was published.] DLC, RPB

610. *Program of the Metropolitan Opera*. The Metropolitan Opera on Tour. [Detroit: Detroit Grand Opera Association.] Vol. 1-. 1959-. Annual. [The last issue held by the Detroit Public Library, in 1967, is the issue for 1966. Thus publication still seems to be in progress.] MiD

611. *Talent*. "For Finer Entertainment" on Stage. New York, New York: Published by MKP, Inc., 116 West 72nd Street. Vol. 3, Nos. 1-2. May 1959, September 1959. [Monthly? I have not been able to discover any other issues of this directory of theatrical agents.] NN (Vol. 3, Nos. 1-2)

612. *The Theatre*. A Weekly Magazine of Drama—Comedy—Music. Edited by Charles H. Lipsett. New York, New York: Atlas Publishing Company, 425 West 25th Street [later, published at 544 West 43rd Street]. Vol. 1, Nos. 1-2. January–December 1959. Then, *The Theatre*. A

Magazine of Drama, Comedy, Music. Vol. 2, No. 1–Vol. 3, No. 9.
January 1960–September 1961. Then, *New York Guide and Theatre
Magazine*. [Absorbed *New York Guide*.] Vol. 3, No. 10–Vol. 4, No.
1. October 1961–January 1962. Monthly. [A specimen copy was is-
sued as Vol. 1, No. 1. 8 November 1958.] CLSU, CLU, CoU, GU, IEN,
IU, IaU, LU, MiD, MoS, MoU, NN (incomplete), OC, OkU, OrU,
PSt, SdU

613. *Theatre Chicago Annual*. Chicago, Illinois: 54 E. Delaware Place. 1959.
Annual. CLSU, FU

614. *The Theatre Magazine: 1959 Yearbook*. New York, New York: Published
by the Atlas Publishing Company, 425 West 25th Street. 1959. Annual. CS, CoU, IU, NN, NjP

615. *Theatre Organ*. Vallejo, California: American Association of Organ En-
thusiasts. No. 1. Spring 1959. [Supersedes *TIBIA*.] DLC

616. *Theatrical Investor*. New York, New York: 130 East 67th Street. Vol. 1,
No. 1. 15 November 1959. Semimonthly. DLC

1960

617. *The American Little Theatre Magazine*. Edited by James Chinello. Los
Angeles, California: P. O. Box No. 49927. Vol. 1, Nos. 1-5. Summer
1960–Autumn 1961. Quarterly. ArU, CSt, CoU, DLC, GU, IEN,
MWelC, NIC, PPiCI

618. *Back Stage*. Edited by Allen Zwerdling. New York, New York: Back
Stage Publications, Inc., 115 West 46th Street. Vols. 1-3, No. 47. [One
hundred issues.] 2 December 1960–28 December 1962. Weekly
(slightly irregular). KyU ([2]–), NN (lacking issues, some mutilated
pages), PPiCI ([2]–)

619. *Billboard*. Overseas Edition. New York, New York: Billboard Publishing
Co. Vol. 1. 2 May–December 1960. Vol. 73–. January 1961–. [The
title varies: *Billboard Music Week*. Overseas Edition. Beginning with
January 1961, assumes the numbering of *Billboard*.] DLC, NN

620. *Broadway Backer*. New York, New York: Published by John P. Beresford,
430 E. 63rd Street. No. 1. 1960. DLC

621. *The California Shavian*. Edited by Eddy S. Feldman. Los Angeles, California: The Shaw Society of California, 1933 South Broadway. Vol. 1–.
January 1960–. Bimonthly. CL, CU, NcU, NIC, NN

622. *The Charles Playbook*. A Project of Playhouse Boston, Inc. Boston, Massachusetts: Published by the Charles Playhouse. Vols. 1-3. 1960/61–
1962/63. Annual. [Vol. 1 says that it will appear twice a year.] DLC,
MH

623. *Coward-McCann Contemporary Drama*. New York, New York: Coward-
McCann, 210 Madison Avenue. No. 1–. 1960–. Irregular. DLC (selective basis), MH (selective basis), MdBJ (selective basis)

24. *Dramatists' Bulletin.* New York, New York: Dramatists Guild. Vols. 1-4, No. 4. October 1960–January 1964. Monthly. [Superseded by *Dramatists Guild Quarterly.*] DLC, NN

25. *Dramatists Play Service, New York, Complete Catalogue of Plays.* New York, New York: 14 E. 38th Street. 1960. Annual. DLC

26. *8:30 Theatre.* Edited by Joyce Morgan (December 1960–January 1961); Jack Norstad (February 1961–January 1962). Minneapolis, Minnesota: 8:30, 3807 Baillif Place. [Vol. 1, Nos. 1-2.] December 1960–January 1961. [Cover title only. No volume or title is listed on the title page.] Then, *8:30.* The Magazine of Twin City Theatre. [Published by 8:30 Publications at 5800 Timberglade Road, February, March, and April 1961, and at Suite 16, Dyckman Hotel, for the remaining issues.] Vol. 1, No. 3–Vol. 2, No. 1. February 1961–January 1962. Monthly. [Eight issues in all. Skipped publication from May through October, 1961.] MnHi

27. *En'core.* The Magazine Community Theatre Magazine. "Edited Exclusively" for the little theatre. Edited by Charles W. Simandl, Jr. Elm Grove, Wisconsin. Vols. 1-4. No. 2. September/October 1960–March/April 1965. Bimonthly (irregular). GU, MH, NN, WaU, WU

28. *New York State Community Theatre Journal.* Edited by Edward J. Mendus. Albany, New York: New York State Community Theatre Association and State University of New York. Vol. 1, No. 1–. December 1960–. Quarterly (irregular). [Supersedes *Community Theatre Bulletin.*] DLC, NN

29. *Opera Society of Washington.* Washington, D.C.: Opera Society of Washington, D.C., 1745 K Street, N.W. 1960/61. [Program.] DLC

30. *Stratford-Upon-Avon Studies.* New York, New York: St. Martin's Press, 175 Fifth Avenue. Vol. 1–. 1960–. Irregular. CLSU, CLU, CU, DLC, ICU, IEN, MB, MdBJ, MH, MiU, NIC, NcD, OrU, OCU, PU, WU

31. *Theatre and Events Guide.* Edited by Peter Moumousis. New York, New York: Theatre & Events Guide, Inc., 570 Fifth Avenue. 1960–. Monthly. [*Standard Periodical Directory*, p. 307.]

32. *Theatre Survey.* An Annual Publication of the American Society for Theatre Research. Edited by Edwin Burr Pettet (1960), Alan Downer (1961-1965), Ralph G. Allen (1966-). Waltham, Massachusetts: Brandeis University. [With Vol. 4, 1963, it began to be published in Pittsburgh, Pennsylvania, at the University of Pittsburgh.] Vols. 1-4. 1960–1963. Annual. Then, *Theatre Survey.* The American Journal of Theatre History. Vol. 5–. 1964–. Semiannual. CSt, KAS, IC, ICN, ICU, MA, MiU, MoSU, NN, NNS, NbU, OU

1961

33. *American Community Theatre Association Newsletter.* Edited by Jeanne

Adams Wray. Washington, D.C.: ACTA, American Educational Theatre Association, Inc., Pennsylvania, N.W. 1961. Bimonthly. DLC (5–, 1964)

634. *Amusement Business.* Combining *The Billboard, Outdoor,* and *Funspot Magazine.* Edited by James W. McHugh. Cincinnati, Ohio: Published by The Billboard Publishing Company, 2160 Patterson Street. Vol. 1, No. 1–. 9 January 1961–. Weekly. [The first issue is also listed as Vol. 73, No. 1, 9 January 1961, a continuation of the numbering of *Billboard.*] DLC, NN

635. *Curtain Call.* Los Angeles Civil Light Opera Association. Los Angeles, California: Playbill, Inc., 8537½ Melrose Avenue. No. 1–. 1961–. Four issues a year. IU (5–)

636. *Drama Survey.* A Review of Dramatic Literature & the Theatrical Arts. Edited by John D. Hurrell. Minneapolis, Minnesota: Published by the Bolingbroke Society, Inc. Printed by the John Roberts Company. Vol. 1–. May 1961–. Three issues a year [later, four issues a year]. ArU, CSt, CU, CoU, CtY, DLC, IEN, IU, InU, MH, MiU, MnU, NjP, NIC, NN, OrU, TxU

637. *First Stage.* Edited by Henry F. Salerno. Lafayette, Indiana: Purdue University, 324 Heavilon Hall. Vol. 1–. Winter 1961/62–. Quarterly. CtY, CSt, CU, DLC, ICU, IU, IaU, LU, MH, MiU, MoU, MnU, NN, NNC, NjP, OU, PSC, PU, TxU

638. *Impressario.* Detroit's Magazine of the Performing Arts. Edited variously by Andy Wilson, Stephen F. Booth, Theodore Seemeyer, and Richard C. Robinson. Detroit, Michigan: 404 Fox Building. Vols. 1-2. October/November 1961–April/May 1963. Then, *Impressario.* Magazine of the Arts. Lathrop Village, Michigan: Village House Publishers, Inc., 28081 Southfield Road. Vol. 3–. Fall 1963–. [Frequency varies from four issues a year to bimonthly.] DLC, MiD, NN

639. *The Leaguer.* Edited by Arthur C. Greene, Jr. Charlottesville, Virginia: School of General Studies, University of Virginia, Madison Hall, University Avenue. Vol. 1–. 1961–. Quarterly (then once a month, September through May). [Amateur theatricals. Supersedes *Virginia Drama News.*] ViU

640. *Playbill/Curtain Call.* Los Angeles, California: 1633 W. 11th Street. 1961. Weekly. [*Standard Periodical Directory,* p. 865.]

641. *Show.* The Magazine of the Performing Arts. Edited by H. Hartford. New York, New York: Hartford Publications, Inc., 140 East 57th Street. Vols. 1-2, No. 3. October 1961–March 1962. Then, *Show.* Incorporating *Show Business Illustrated.* The Magazine of the Performing Arts. Vol. 2, No. 4–Vol. 5, No. 3. May 1962–April 1965. Monthly. [Absorbed *Show Business Illustrated,* May 1962. Some issues lack the

subtitle.] ArU, CLU, CoU, DLC, GU, IU, MdBJ, MoS, NN, NNC, NjP, OC, PU, WU

42. *Show Business Illustrated* (*SBI*). Edited by Hugh M. Hefner. Chicago, Illinois: HMH Publishing Company, Inc., 232 E. Ohio Street. Vols. 1-2, No. 4. 5 September 1961–April 1962. [Twelve issues.] Biweekly (September 1961–January 1962 [not published December 1961]); monthly (February–April 1962). [November 1961–April 1962, the title is *SBI: Show Business Illustrated.* Merged with *Show* May 1962.] DeU, DLC, IU, MiD, NN, NjP

43. *Young Playgoers.* The American Theatre for Children. Edited by Barbara Fisher. New York, New York: 71 West 10th Street. Vol. 1, No. 1. November 1961. [The Library of Congress says that it did not retain its copy.]

1962

44. *Dance-Music-Drama in the New York City Park System.* New York, New York: Issued by the Department of Parks of New York City. Summer 1962–. Irregular. NN

45. *The Dunster Drama Review.* Edited by Lance Morrow (9 March 1962–22 March 1963); Travis J. Williams (18 October–6 December 1963); Mark Coleman (7 February–8 May 1964). Cambridge, Massachusetts: Harvard University, Dunster House. Vols. 1-3, No. 9. 9 March 1962–8 May 1964. Published occasionally. [Twenty-five issues. Mimeographed.] MH (missing Vol. 1, No. 2, and Vol. 2, No. 4)

46. *Footlight.* Washington, D.C.: John F. Kennedy Center for the Performing Arts, 718 Jackson Place, N.W. No. 1–. July 1962–. Monthly. CU, DLC, IC, OU, WM

47. *Independent Shavians.* New York, New York: New York Shavians, Inc., c/o Apt. 5E, 14 Washing Place. [Vol. 1]–. October 1962–. Three issues a year. CLSU, DLC, IaU, NIC, NN, OU

48. *Musical Show.* Devoted to the Amateur Presentation of Broadway Musical Shows on the Stage. Edited by Robert Asborn Hut. New York, New York: Tams-Witmark Music Library, Inc., 115 West 45th Street. [Vol. 1]–. 1962–. Three times a year. [Amateur theatricals. Distributed free.] CoFS, NN

49. *Playbill.* Edited by Walter Wager (Vol. 1, No. 3–. March 1964–). San Francisco, California: Playbill Incorporated, 485 Brannan Street. Vol. 1, No. 1–Vol. 1, No. 50. 31 December 1962–9 December 1963. [New numbering.] Vol. 1–. January 1964–. Weekly (to 9 December 1963), monthly (January 1964–). [The most recent version at the University of California, Berkeley, is Vol. 3, No. 2. February 1966. Various ver-

sions of each issue. Some issues published by Playbill of Southern Califorina, Inc., 8537½ Melrose Ave., Los Angeles, California. Then, New York, New York: Playbill, Inc., 579 Fifth Avenue.] CU

650. *Playwrights Newsletter.* Edited by Aubrey Hampton. New York, New York: The Playwrights Circle, 225 Lafayette Street. Vol. 1, Nos. 1-2. 28 February–28 March 1962. Monthly (except June, July, and August). [The University of Georgia librarian states that the publisher canceled the subscription after the second issue and refunded the money. Presumably there were no further issues published.] CLSU, GU

651. *Script.* New York, New York: Published by the Lambs Club. Summer 1962–. Quarterly (irregular). [Supersedes *Lambs Script.*] NN

652. *17th and 18th Century Theatre Research.* Edited by Carl J. Stratman, C.S.V., and David G. Spencer. Chicago, Illinois: Loyola University, 6525 N. Sheridan Road. Vol. 1, Nos. 1-2. May–November 1962. Then, *Restoration and 18th Century Theatre Research.* Vol. 2–. May 1963–. Semiannual. ICL, ICN, MB, MH, NN, NNC, OU

653. *Southern Sawdust.* Edited by L. Wilson Poarch. Arlington, Virginia: Robert D. Vandiford, Jr., Mimeo Press, 835 Falls Road, Rocky Mount, North Carolina. Nos. 1-22. 2 May 1962–14 August 1967. Quarterly. [My information on the magazine comes from Princeton University.] NjP

654. *The Theatrical News.* A Newspaper for the Regional and Educational Theatres of America. Edited by Bernard Simon. New York, New York: Published by Package Publicity Service, 247 West 46th Street. Vol. 1, No. 1. 5 February 1962. [The Library of Congress says that it did not retain its copy.]

1963

655. *ANTA News Bulletin.* Edited by Ruth M. Mayleas. New York, New York: Published by the American National Theatre and Academy, 1545 Broadway [later, 247 West 52nd Street]. Vol. 1, No. 1–. October 1963–. Irregular. [Supersedes *ANTA Newsletter.*] CLU, IU, MH, NN, PPiU

656. *Harvard Drama Review.* Edited by Alan Mason, and Jan Broek. Cambridge, Massachusetts: Harvard University. Vol. 1, Nos. 1-7. 25 October 1963–8 May 1964. [Mimeographed. To review productions at the Loeb Drama Center.] MH

657. *The Secondary School Theatre Conference News.* Edited by David Cropp. Washington, D.C.: Secondary School Theatre Conference, American Educational Theatre Association, Inc., 1701 Pennsylvania Avenue, N.W. 1963. Triannual. [*Standard Periodical Directory,* p. 865.]

1964

58. *American National Theatre and Academy Report.* New York, New York. 1964. Annual. MH

59. *Ante.* Edited by William Harris. Los Angeles, California: Echo Press, Box 29915. No. 1–. Summer 1964–. Quarterly. CLSU, CLU, CU, DLC, IEN, LNHT, MH, NN, OrU, TxHR, WaU

60. *Curtain Playwrights.* Chicago, Illinois: University of Chicago Press. No. 1–. 1964–. Irregular. ICU, KU, MB

61. *Dance Year.* Dance Spotlight. Boston, Massachusetts: 1330 Commonwealth Avenue. 1964–. Annual. ArU, AzU, C, CL, CSf, GU, IU, MiU, MoS, NIC, NN, NNC, NhU, WU

62. *The Dramatists Guild Quarterly.* Edited by Otis L. Guernsey, Jr. New York, New York: Issued by the Dramatists' Guild of the Authors' League of America, Inc., 6 East 39th Street. Vol. 1–. Spring 1964–. Quarterly. DLC, IU (2–), NN (last issue is Vol. 2, No. 1, Spring 1965?), WU ([3]–)

63. *Folk Music Yearbook of Artists.* Jandel Productions International. Fairfax, Virginia. Vol. 1–. 1964–. Annual. CoD, DLC, IU, NN

64. *Lincoln Center New York State Theatre Program.* Lincoln Center for the Performing Arts, New York. New York State Theatre. New York, New York: Saturday Review, Inc., 25 W. 45th Street. 20 April 1964–. Irregular. [Programs for 20 April 1964–. Called also Inaugural Performances.] NN

65. *The Players Showcase.* Movies, Television, Cabaret, Records. Edited by Lawrence Teeman. Skokie, Illinois: Publishers' Development Corporation, 8150 N. Central Park Avenue. Vol. 1, Nos. 1-3. Fall 1964– Spring 1965. Quarterly. DLC, NN

66. *Puppetry Guild of Greater New York, Inc., Newsletter.* Edited by Anne-Marie Cecil. New York, New York: c/o Frank Paris, 12 Gay Street. 1964. Bimonthly. [*Standard Periodical Directory*, p. 865.]

67. *Religious Theatre.* Modern Religious Theatre Movement. Edited by James R. Carlson and Warren Kliewer. Saint Petersburg, Florida: c/o James R. Carlson, Florida Presbyterian College. Vol. 1, No. 1–. 1964–. DLC, IaU, MH, NN, WaU (2–)

68. *S-B Gazette.* Sausalito-Belvedere. Edited by Leon Spiro. Sausalito, California: Box 731. 1964. Quarterly. [Text in English, French, German, Italian, Portuguese, and Spanish; summaries in English.] [*Ulrich's International Periodicals Directory*, Second Annual Supplement, 1967 (New York and London, 1967), p. 54.]

69. *Setting the Stage.* Minneapolis, Minnesota: Minnesota Theatre Company, 725 Vineland Place. 1964–. Annual. [The Tyrone Guthrie Theatre.] WM

70. *Souvenir Magazine of Broadway.* Edited by Nat Dorfman. New York,

New York: Souvenir Book of Broadway, 250 West 57th Street. 1964. Quarterly. [*Standard Periodical Directory*, p. 865.]

671. *Theatre.* The Annual of the Repertory Theatre of Lincoln Center. Edited by Barry Hyams. New York, New York: A Repertory Theatre Publication in Association with Playbill, Inc. [1965, published by Hill and Wang.] Vol. 1. 1964–. Annual. CU, CtW, DLC, DeU, MH, MdBJ, NN, NNC, WaU

1965

672. *Afro-Asian Theatre Bulletin.* The Newsletter of the A.E.T.A. Afro-Asian Theatre Project. Edited by Frederic M. Litto. Lawrence, Kansas: University of Kansas, Department of Speech and Drama. Vol. 1–. October 1965–. [Mimeographed.] CU, CtY, InU, KU

673. *Children's Theatre News.* Pleasantville, New York: Region 14, Children's Theatre Conference. c/o M. D. Ostrander, 48 Cedar Avenue. 1965. Three times a year. [*Standard Periodical Directory*, p. 864.]

674. *Choragos.* The Leader of the Chorus. Denver, Colorado: Verb Publications, 1323 E. 14th Street. Vol. 1, No. 1. April 1965. Bimonthly. [Publishes plays for small theater productions, especially poetic drama. See *Bulletin of Bibliography*, XXIV (January/April 1964), 134.]

675. *Fine Arts Monthly.* Edited by Clark Smile. Amarillo, Texas: Publisher, Clark Smile, 1312 Smiley Street. Vol. 1, No. 1. 1965.

676. *Intermission Magazine.* Edited by Gene Cole. Chicago, Illinois: Intermission Press, 3179 N. Broadway Avenue. 1965. Monthly. [*Ulrich's International Periodicals Directory*, Second Annual Supplement, 1967, p. 93.]

677. *SRO: Shakespeare Research Opportunities.* The Report of the Modern Language Association of America Conference. Edited by W. R. Elton. Riverside, California: Published by the Department of English, University of California at Riverside. No. 1–. 1965–. Annual. [Mimeographed.] CLU, CU, DLC, ICU, IU, MH, MiU, NN, NNC

678. *Shakespeare Studies.* Edited by J. Leeds Barroll III. Cincinnati, Ohio: University of Cincinnati. No. 1–. October 1965–. Annual. DFo, DLC, ICN, ICU, MH, NIC, NN, PU, TxU

679. *Theatre Design and Technology.* Journal of the United States Institute for Theatre Technology. Edited by Ned A. Bowman. Pittsburgh, Pennsylvania: University of Pittsburgh. No. 1–. May 1965–. Quarterly. C, CLSU, CoU, GU, ICU, IU, IaU, KyU, MeB, NjP, NjR, OrU

1966

680. *Opera Company of Boston.* Opera Guide. Boston, Massachusetts. 1966–. Annual. DLC

31. *Something Else Newsletter.* Edited by Roscommon Pike. New York, New York: 160 Fifth Avenue. February 1966–. Six issues a year. [Free.]

1967

32. *Comparative Drama.* Kalamazoo, Michigan: Western Michigan University. Vol. 1, No. 1–. March 1967. Quarterly. CU, DLC, GU, IU, MH, MoU, NIC, NjP, PU, ViU, WU

33. *Critic's Guide to Movies and Plays.* Edited by Edwin S. Finkelstein. New York, New York: 213 E. 84th Street. 1967. Bimonthly. [*Ulrich's International Periodicals Directory*, Second Annual Supplement, 1967, p. 69.]

34. *Modern International Drama.* University Park, Pennsylvania: Penn State University Press, University Press Building. No. 1–. September 1967–. Semiannual. [*Bulletin of Bibliography*, XXV (September/December 1967), 85.]

35. *Theatre Crafts.* Emmaus, Pennsylvania: 33 E. Minor Street. No. 1–. March 1967–. Bimonthly. [*Bulletin of Bibliography*, XXV (May/August 1967), 68.]

Addenda

1839

The Corsair. A Gazette of Literature, Art, Dramatic Criticism, Fashion and Novelty. Edited by N. P. Willis, and T. O. Porter. New York, New York. Vol. 1, Nos. 1-52. 16 March 1839–7 March 1840. Weekly. CSmH, CtY, DLC, ICN, ICU, IU, MB, MH, MiU, NN, NNC, NjR, OC, ViU, WHi, WU

1843

The Anglo American. A Journal of Literature, News, Politics, the Drama, Fine Arts, etc. Edited by A. D. Paterson. New York, New York: E. L. Garvin & Co. Vols. 1-10, No. 4. 29 April 1843–13 November 1847. Weekly. [Merged into *Albion.*] DLC, ICN ([1-8]), MH (1-9), MnU, NN (1-2, [4]-10), NNC (1-9), NNS (2-10)

1901

Theater Zshurnal. New York, New York. Vols. 1-2, [Nos. 1-15]. 1 October 1901–1 May 1902. Biweekly. CtY, DLC, NN, WHi

1902

Echo. A Magazine Devoted to Society, Literature, and Stage in the South. Richmond, Virginia. Vol. 1, No. 1. 15 February 1902. ViU

1905

Theater Zinger. New York, New York. Nos. 1-5. 1 July 1905–15 January 1909. Irregular. [In Yiddish.] NN

1913

Theater un Muving Piktshurs. New York, New York. Vol. 1, Nos. 1-9. 17 October–12 December 1913. Weekly. [In Yiddish. The English title is *Theatre and Moving Picture Review.*] DLC, NN

1930

The Players Bulletin. New York, New York: For the Players Club, 16 Gramercy Park. [Vol. 1–.] April 1930–. Quarterly (very irregular). [Devoted primarily to the activities of the Players Club. No issues are numbered.] NN

1932

irginia Drama News. Charlottesville, Virginia: Published by the University of Virginia Extension Department, with the cooperation of the Virginia Players (September 1932–November 1942). Vols. 1-29, No. 8. 15 September 1932–May 1961. Irregular (published from five to eight times a year). [Mimeographed. Devoted to amateur theatricals. Edited variously by Miss Roy Land, Roger Boyle, and Margaret Huffman.] NN, ViU

1946

agic Is Fun. An Independent Magazine for the Amateur Magician. New York, New York. Nos. 1-7. March/April 1946–October/December 1947. Bimonthly. DLC, NN

References

merican Book Trade Directory. New York: R. R. Bowker, 1915–. [One issue every three years.]

merican Newspapers 1821–1936: A Union List of Files Available in the United States and Canada. Edited by Winifred Gregory. New York: H. W. Wilson, 1937. [Continues Brigham's work.]

merican Periodical Series: 1800-1850. Ann Arbor, Michigan: University Microfilms, 1947–.

Ayer's Directory] N. W. Ayer and Son's Directory of Newspapers and Periodicals. Philadelphia: N. W. Ayer and Son, 1880–. [Annual.]

ibliography of Foreign Language and Newspapers and Periodicals Published in Chicago. Chicago: Chicago Public Library Omnibus Project, Works Project Administration, 1942. [Mimeographed.]

Births and Deaths in the Periodical World," Bulletin of Bibliography. 1897–. [Each issue.]

righam, Clarence S. History and Bibliography of American Newspapers, 1690-1820. Worcester, Massachusetts: American Antiquarian Society, 1947. 2 vols.

annons, Harry G. T. Classified Guide to 1700 Annuals, Directories, Calendars, and Year Books. New York: H. W. Wilson, 1923. 196 pp.

Catalogue of the Allen A. Brown Collection of Books Relating to the Stage in the Public Library of the City of Boston. Boston: Trustees of the Public Library of the City of Boston, 1919. 952 pp.

ilmer, Gertrude C. Checklist of Southern Periodicals to 1861. Boston: F. W. Faxon, 1934.

ohdes, Clarence. Literature and Theatre of the States and Regions of the U.S.A. Durham, North Carolina: Duke University Press, 1967. 276 pp.

regory, Winifred. American Newspapers, 1821-1936. New York: H. W. Wilson, 1937. 791 pp.

riffin, Max L. "A Bibliography of New Orleans Magazines," Louisiana Historical Quarterly, XVIII (July 1935), 491-556.

offman, Frederick J., Allen, Charles, and Ulrich, Carolyn F. The Little Magazine: A History and a Bibliography. Princeton, New Jersey: Princeton University Press, 1946. 440 pp.

omer, Thomas J. A Guide to Serial Publications in the Libraries of Boston, Cambridge, and Vicinity. Boston: Cooperating Committee, 1922-1956. 779 pp.

ott, Frank L. A History of American Magazines. Vol. 1: 1741-1850; Vol. 2: 1850-1865; Vol. 3: 1865-1885; Vol. 4: 1885-1905. Cambridge, Massachusetts: Harvard University Press, 1930-1957. 4 vols.

New Serial Titles. Washington, D.C.: Library of Congress, 1953–. [Monthly, with annual cumulation.]

New Serial Titles, 1950-1960. Supplement to the *Union List of Serials.* Third edition. Washington, D.C.: Library of Congress, 1961. 2 vols.

New Serial Titles, 1961 Cumulation. Washington, D.C.: Library of Congress, 1962. 867 pp.

New Serial Titles, 1962 Cumulation. Washington, D.C.: Library of Congress, 1963. 1341 pp.

New Serial Titles, 1963 Cumulation. Washington, D.C.: Library of Congress, 1964. 2035 pp.

New Serial Titles, 1964 Cumulation. Washington, D.C.: Library of Congress, 1965. 2 vols.

New Serial Titles, 1961-1965 Cumulation. New York and London: R. R. Bowker; New York: Arno, 1966. 2 vols.

New Serial Titles, 1966 Cumulation. Washington, D.C.: Library of Congress, 1967. 935 pp.

Newspapers in Libraries of Chicago. A Joint Check List. Chicago: University of Chicago Libraries, 1936. 258 pp.

Scott, Franklin William. *Newspapers and Periodicals of Illinois, 1814-1879.* Revised and enlarged edition. Springfield, Illinois: Trustees of the Illinois State Historical Library, 1910. 610 pp. [Vol. 6 in Collections of the Illinois State Library. Bibliographical Series, Vol. 1.]

Severance, Henry O. *A Guide to the Current Periodicals and Serials of the United States and Canada.* Fifth edition. Ann Arbor, Michigan: George Wahr, 1931. 432 pp.

The Standard Periodical Directory, 1967. Second edition. New York: Oxbridge, 1967. 1019 pp.

Stock, Leo F. *A List of American Periodicals and Serial Publications in the Humanities and Social Sciences.* Washington, D.C.: American Council of Learned Societies, 1934. 130 pp.

[Ulrich, Carolyn F.] *Ulrich's Periodicals Directory.* Ninth edition. Edited by Eileen C. Graves. New York, New York: R. R. Bowker, 1959. 716 pp. [See also: first edition, 1932; second edition, 1935; third edition, 1938; fourth edition, 1943; fifth edition, 1947; sixth edition, 1951; seventh edition, 1953; eighth edition, 1956.]

Union List of Little Magazines. Chicago: Midwest Inter-Library Center, 1956.

Union List of Serials in Libraries of the United States and Canada. Second edition. Edited by Winifred Gregory. New York: H. W. Wilson, 1943. 3065 pp. [Original edition in 1927.]

———. Second edition. Supplement. January 1941–December 1943. Edited by Gabrielle E. Malikoff. New York: H. W. Wilson, 1945. 1123 pp.

———. Second edition. Second Supplement. January 1944–December 1949. Edited by Marga Franck. New York: H. W. Wilson, 1953. 1365 pp.

————. Third edition. Edited by Edna Brown Titus. New York: H. W. Wilson, 1965. 5 vols.

Wescott, Mary, and Ramage, Allene. *A Checklist of United States Newspapers and Weeklies before 1900 in the General Library* [of Duke University]. Durham, North Carolina: Duke University, 1932-1937. 6 parts.

Publication Spans of Theatrical Periodicals

All periodicals included in this bibliography that had a publication span of more than one year are listed below. These charts are designed to enable the reader who is interested in the theater in a certain period to determine which theatrical periodicals were published during that time. Each publication is listed by entry number and abbreviated title. A † at the beginning of a twenty-year period indicates that a periodical was published during the previous twenty-year period and is shown on the preceding chart, and a † at the end of a period shows that publication continued and the periodical is listed on the succeeding chart.

1805-1824	1805	1806	1807	1808	1809	1810	1811	1812	1813	1814	1815	1816	1817	1818	1819	1820	1821	1822	1823	1824
2 Theatrical Censor	*	*																		
3 Thespian Mirror	*	*																		
5 Rambler's Magazine					*	*														
7 Mirror of Taste						*	*													
9 Comet							*	*												
12 Boston Weekly													*	*	*	*				*
13 Theatrical Budget																				*

1825-1844	1825	1826	1827	1828	1829	1830	1831	1832	1833	1834	1835	1836	1837	1838	1839	1840	1841	1842	1843	1844
13 Theatrical Budget	*																			
15 Critic	*	*																		
19 Euterpeiad				*	*															
20 Spirit of the Times							*	*	*	*	*	*	*	*	*	*	*	*	*	* †
23 Gentleman's Vade-Mecum									*	*										
24 Dramatic Mirror																	*	*		
25 Lorgnette																	*	*	*	

1845-1864	1845	1846	1847	1848	1849	1850	1851	1852	1853	1854	1855	1856	1857	1858	1859	1860	1861	1862	1863	1864
20 Spirit of the Times	†	*	*	*	*	*	*	*	*	*	*	*	*	*	*	*	*	*	*	*
27 Entr'acte				*	*															
28 Figaro				*	*															
32 New York Clipper							*	*	*	*	*	*	*	*	*	*	*	*	*	* †
34 Loge d'Opera									*	*										
35 Porter's Spirit of Times											*	*	*	*	*	*				
37 Lorgnette												*	*	*						
38 Wilkes' Spirit of Times												*	*	*	*	*	*		*	* †
39 Daily Dramatic Review														*	*					
40 Programme																*	*	*	*	†
41 Daily Dramatic News																				†

1865-1884

	1865	1866	1867	1868	1869	1870	1871	1872	1873	1874	1875	1876	1877	1878	1879	1880	1881	1882	1883	1884
32 New York Clipper	†	*	*	*	*	*	*	*	*	*	*	*	*	*	*	*	*	*	*	†
38 Wilkes' Spirit of Times	†	*	*	*	*	*	*	*	*	*	*	*	*	*	*	*	*	*	*	†
40 Programme	†	*	*	*	*	*	*	*	*											
41 Daily Dramatic News	†																			
42 Daily Dramatic Chron.	*	*	*	*	*															
43 Stage	*	*	*	*	*	*	*	*	*	*	*	*	*	*	*	*	*			
45 Prompter		*	*																	
47 Daily Critic		*	*																	
48 Opera House Programme		*	*	*	*															
49 Sport. Times		*	*	*	*	*	*													
50 Critic							*	*												
52 Season							*	*	*											
53 Folio							*	*	*	*	*	*	*	*	*	*	*	*	*	†
54 Ladies The. Bouquet							*	*												
56 Figaro								*	*	*	*	*	*	*	*	*	*	*	*	†
57 Season								*	*											
59 Boston Ray									*	*	*									
60 American Athenæum									*	*										
61 Arcadian									*	*	*	*	*	*						
62 Dexter Smith's Paper									*	*	*	*	*	*						
63 Echo											*	*								
65 N.Y. Clipper Annual												*	*	*	*	*	*	*	†	
66 Brooklyn Daily Stage												*	*	*	*	*				
67 Music Trade Review												*	*	*	*	*	*	*		
68 N.Y. Dramatic News												*	*	*	*	*	*	*	*	*
70 N.Y. Illustrated Times														*	*	*	*	*	*	*
71 Play-Bill														*	*					
72 Illus. Drama & Sport															*	*				
74 Warrington's															*	*	*	*	*	*
76 New York Figaro																*	*	*	*	†
77 New York Mirror																*	*	*	*	†
78 Dramatic Magazine																*	*	*		
80 Byrne's Dramatic Times																*	*	*	†	
81 Critic																*	*	*	†	
83 Stage																*	*			
84 Theatrical Guide																	*	*		
85 Music																		*	*	
88 Freund's Music & Drama																			*	†
89 Keynote																			*	†
90 Musical Observer																			*	*
91 Oriole Tidings																			*	†
92 Shakespeariana																			*	†
94 Harry Miner's Directory																				†

1885-1904

	1885	1886	1887	1888	1889	1890	1891	1892	1893	1894	1895	1896	1897	1898	1899	1900	1901	1902	1903	1904
32 New York Clipper	†	*	*	*	*	*	*	*	*	*	*	*	*	*	*	*	*	*	*	†
38 Wilkes' Spirit of Times	†	*	*	*	*	*	*	*	*	*	*	*	*	*	*	*	*	*	*	
53 Folio	†	*	*	*	*	*	*	*	*	*										
56 Figaro	†	*	*	*	*	*	*	*	*	*	*	*	*	*	*	*	*	*	*	*
65 N.Y. Clipper Annual	†	*	*	*	*	*	*	*	*	*	*	*	*	*	*	*	*			
68 N.Y. Dramatic News	†	*	*	*	*	*	*	*	*	*	*	*	*	*	*	*	*	*	*	†
76 New York Figaro	†	*	*	*	*	*	*	*	*	*	*	*	*	*	*	*				

1885-1904 *(cont.)*

No.	Title	1885	1886	1887	1888	1889	1890	1891	1892	1893	1894	1895	1896	1897	1898	1899	1900	1901	1902	1903	1904
77	New York Mirror	†	*	*	*	*	*	*	*	*	*	*	*	*	*	*	*	*	*	*	†
80	Byrne's Dramatic Times	†	*	*	*	*	*	*	*	*	*	*	*								
81	Critic	†	*	*	*	*	*	*	*	*	*	*	*	*	*	*	*	*	*	*	†
88	Freund's Music & Drama	†	*	*	*	*	*	*	*												
89	Keynote	†	*	*	*	*	*	*	*	*	*	*	*	*							
91	Oriole Tidings	†	*																		
92	Shakespeariana	†	*	*	*	*	*	*	*	*	*										
95	Dramatic News	†	*	*	*																
94	Harry Miner's Directory	*	*																		
96	N.Y. Amusement Gazette	*	*	*	*	*	*	*	*	*											
97	Shakespeare Society	*	*	*	*	*	*	*	*	*	*	*	*	*	*	*	*	*	*	*	†
99	Theatre	*	*	*	*	*	*	*	*												
104	Stage				*	*	*														
105	Amusement Bulletin				*	*															
108	N.Y. Saturday Review				*	*	*														
109	Poet Lore				*	*	*	*	*	*	*	*	*	*	*	*	*	*	*	*	†
110	Dramatic Mirror Quart.					*	*														
111	Philadelphia Music					*	*	*													
114	At Home & Abroad						*	*	*	*	*										
115	Amusement Globe						*	*													
116	Cleveland Amusement								*	*	*	*	*								
117	Dramatic Chronicle								*	*											
118	Dramatic Studies								*	*			*	*	*						
119	Opera								*	*	*										
120	Billboard								*	*	*	*	*	*	*	*	*	*	†		
121	Gallery of Players									*	*	*	*								
123	N.Y. Dramatic Chronicle									*	*	*									
124	Opera									*	*										
125	Opera Glass									*	*	*	*	*							
126	Shakespeare									*	*										
127	Shakespeariana Club									*	*										
128	Am. Shakespeare Mag.										*	*	*	*							
129	Footlights										*	*									
131	Mahatma										*	*	*	*	*	*	*	*	*	†	
132	Stage										*	*									
134	Cahn-Leighton Guide												*	*	*	*	*	*	*	*	†
135	Lyceum Night												*	*	*	*	*	*	*	*	†
137	Critic														*	*					
138	Dramatic Magazine														*	*	*	*	*	*	
139	Amusement Record														*	*					
140	Broadway Magazine													*	*	*	*	*	†		
141	Actors Society													*	*	*	*	*	†		
142	Cast													*	*	*	*	*	†		
143	Dramatic Review													*	*						
144	Elite													*	*	*	*				
145	Impressionist													*	*						
146	Opera Glass													*	*						
148	San Francisco Drama													*	*	*	*	*	†		
149	Magician														*	*	*				
150	Our Players Gallery													*	*	*	*	†			
151	San Francisco Guide														*	*	*				
154	Music & Stage															*	*				
155	New Shakespeareana															*	*	*	†		

1885-1904 (cont.)

No.	Title	1901	1902	1903	1904
158	"Tricks"	*	*	*	
162	Sphinx	*	*		†
163	Theatre Journal	*	*		†
166	Bull. Nat. Art Theatre			*	†
167	Burr McIntosh Monthly			*	†
168	Drama			*	†
171	New Alcazar			*	†
172	New York Inquirer			*	*
173	Philadelphia The. Guide			*	*
176	Iconoclast				†
177	New York Playhouses				†
178	Stage				†

1905-1924

No.	Title	1905	1906	1907	1908	1909	1910	1911	1912	1913	1914	1915	1916	1917	1918	1919	1920	1921	1922	1923	1924
32	New York Clipper	†	*	*	*	*	*	*	*	*	*	*	*	*	*	*	*	*	*	*	*
68	N.Y. Dramatic News	†	*	*	*	*	*	*	*	*	*	*	*	*							
77	New York Mirror	†	*	*	*	*	*	*	*	*	*	*	*								
81	Critic	†	*																		
97	Shakespeare Society	†	*	*	*	*	*	*	*	*	*	*	*	*	*	*	*	*	*	*	†
109	Poet Lore	†	*	*	*	*	*	*	*	*	*	*	*	*	*	*	*	*	*	*	†
120	Billboard	†	*	*	*	*	*	*	*	*	*	*	*	*	*	*	*	*	*	*	†
131	Mahatma	†	*																		
134	Cahn-Leighton Guide	†	*	*	*	*	*	*	*	*	*	*	*	*	*	*	*	*			
135	Lyceum Night	†																			
140	Broadway Magazine	†	*	*	*	*	*	*	*												
141	Actors Society	†	*	*	*																
142	Cast	†	*	*	*	*	*	*	*	*	*	*	*	*	*	*	*	*	*	†	
148	San Francisco Drama	†	*	*	*	*	*	*	*	*	*										
150	Our Players Gallery	†	*	*	*	*	*	*	*	*	*	*	*	*	*	*	*	*	*	*	†
155	New Shakespeareana	†	*	*	*	*	*														
162	Sphinx	†	*	*	*	*	*	*	*	*	*	*	*	*	*	*	*	*	*	*	†
166	Bull. Nat. Art Theatre	†																			
167	Burr McIntosh Monthly	†	*	*	*	*	*														
168	Drama	†																			
171	New Alcazar	†	*	*	*	*															
176	Iconoclast	†	*																			
177	New York Playhouses	†																				
178	Stage	†	*																			
183	Show	*	*	*	*																
184	Variety	*	*	*	*	*	*	*	*	*	*	*	*	*	*	*	*	*	*	*	†
186	Am. Inter. Musical	*	*	*	*	*	*	*													
187	Conjurer's Monthly	*	*	*																	
189	Green Room Book	*	*	*	*																
190	Modern Theatre	*	*																		
193	St. Louis Dramatic News	*	*	*	*																
197	Art World	*	*																		
198	Crest Magician	*	*																		
199	Crest Musical Bulletin	*	*																		
202	Show World	*	*	*	*	*															
203	Theatre	*	*	*	*	*	*														
208	New York Star		*	*	*	*	*	*	*	*	*	*	*	*	*	*	*	*	*	*	†

1905-1924 (cont.)

	1905	1906	1907	1908	1909	1910	1911	1912	1913	1914	1915	1916	1917	1918	1919	1920	1921	1922	1923	1924
209 Theater Welt	*	*																		
211 Boy Magician		*	*	*	*															
213 Dramatist		*	*	*	*	*	*	*	*	*	*	*	*	*	*	*	*	*	*	†
214 Edward's Monthly		*	*																	
215 Green Book Album		*	*	*	*															
216 Idishe Bihne	*	*																		
219 Opera News		*	*	*	*	*	*	*	*	*	*	*								
220 Player		*	*	*	*	*	*	*	*	*										
225 Drama League N.Y.				*	*	*	*	*												
226 Drama League Chi.				*	*	*	*													
230 Magic	*	*																		
231 Opera House Reporter		*	*	*	*	*	*	*	*	*	*	*								
234 Castle Square				*	*	*	*	*	*											
236 Drama				*	*	*	*	*	*	*	*	*	*	*	*	*	*	*	†	
237 Drama League Boston				*	*	*	*	*	*	*	*									
239 M-U-M					*	*	*	*	*	*	*	*	*	*	*	*	*	*	*	†
240 The. Weekly Record					*	*	*													
241 Tip Folio					*	*	*	*	*	*	*									
242 What's Going On					*	*	*	*	*	*	*	*	*	*	*	*	*	*	*	†
243 American Playwright					*	*	*	*												
244 Drama League Wash.							*	*	*	*	*									
249 Conjuring Record							*	*	*											
251 Drama League N.Y.							*	*	*	*	*	*								
253 Foyer							*	*	*											
256 Play-Book							*	*	*											
259 Bull. Catholic The.									*	*	*	*	*	*	*	*	*	*	*	†
260 Gus Hill's Directory									*	*										
261 Inter. Music & Drama									*	*	*									
262 Little Review									*	*	*	*	*	*	*	*	*	*	*	†
263 Magical Bulletin									*	*	*	*	*	*	*	*	*	*	*	†
264 Opera Magazine								*	*	*										
266 Eagle Magician									*	*	*	*	*	*	*	*				
267 Equity									*	*	*	*	*	*	*	*	*	*	*	†
269 N.Y. Dramatic Chron.									*	*	*	*								
271 Drama League Monthly										*	*	*	*							
274 Holmes' Trade Sheet										*	*	*	*	*						
275 Outlaw										*	*									
276 Theatre Arts											*	*	*	*	*	*	*	*	*	†
278 Magic World											*	*	*	*	*	*	*	*	*	*
279 Prompter											*	*								
282 Drama League Calendar													*	*	*	*	*	*	†	
284 Club Chatter													*	*						
286 Critic													*	*						
287 Felsman's Review													*	*	*	*	*	†		
288 Shadowland													*	*	*	*	*			
292 Billboard's Index														*	*	*	*	†		
295 Little Theatres														*	*	*	*	*		
296 New York Star														*	*	*	*	†		
300 Stage														*	*	*	†			
302 Cue														*	*	*	†			
303 Music Record														*	*	*	*			
304 Pantomime														*	*					
305 Play List														*	*	*	†			

1905-1924 (cont.)

	1921	1922	1923	1924
306 Playlist N.Y. Drama	*	*	*	*
308 Zit's Weekly	*	*	*	†
310 N.Y. Dramatic Chron.		*	*	†
312 Theatre & School		*	*	†
313 Dance Lovers Magazine			*	†
315 Theatre Guild Bulletin			*	†
317 Chicago & Mid-West				†
318 Denishawn Magazine				†
321 Greenwich Playbill				†
322 Jewish Theatrical News				†
323 Little Theatre Monthly				†
324 Little Theatre News				†
325 Little Theatre Play List				†
327 N.Y. Amusements				†
328 Players Magazine				†
329 Shakespeare Assoc. Bull.				†

1925-1944

	1925	1926	1927	1928	1929	1930	1931	1932	1933	1934	1935	1936	1937	1938	1939	1940	1941	1942	1943	1944
97 Shakespeare Society	†	*																		
109 Poet Lore	†	*	*	*	*	*	*	*	*	*	*	*	*	*	*	*	*	*	*	†
120 Billboard	†	*	*	*	*	*	*	*	*	*	*	*	*	*	*	*	*	*	*	†
142 Cast	†	*	*	*	*	*	*	*	*	*	*	*	*	*	*	*	*	*	*	†
150 Our Players Gallery	†	*	*	*	*	*	*													
162 Sphinx	†	*	*	*	*	*	*	*	*	*	*	*	*	*	*	*	*	*	†	
184 Variety	†	*	*	*	*	*	*	*	*	*	*	*	*	*	*	*	*	*	*	†
208 New York Star	†	*																		
213 Dramatist	†	*	*	*	*	*	*	*												
236 Drama	†	*	*	*	*	*	*													
239 M-U-M	†	*	*																	
242 What's Going On	†	*	*	*	*	*	*	*												
259 Bull. Catholic The.	†	*	*	*	*	*	*	*												
262 Little Review	†	*	*	*	*															
263 Magical Bulletin	†																			
267 Equity	†	*	*	*	*	*	*	*	*	*	*	*	*	*	*	*	*	*	*	†
276 Theatre Arts	†	*	*	*	*	*	*	*	*	*	*	*	*	*	*	*	*	*	*	†
282 Drama League Calendar	†	*	*	*	*															
287 Felsman's Review	†	*	*	*	*	*	*													
292 Billboard's Index	†	*	*	*	*	*	*	*	*	*	*	*	*	*	*	*				
296 New York Star	†	*	*	*	*	*														
302 Cue	†	*	*	*	*	*	*	*	*	*	*	*	*	*	*	*	*	*	*	†
305 Play List	†																			
310 N.Y. Dramatic Chron.	†	*	*	*	*	*	*	*	*	*	*	*								
308 Zit's Weekly	†	*																		
312 Theatre & School	†	*	*	*	*	*	*	*	*	*	*	*								
313 Dance Lovers Magazine	†	*	*	*	*	*	*													
315 Theatre Guild Bulletin	†	*	*	*	*	*	*	*	*	*	*	*	*							
317 Chicago & Mid-West	†																			
318 Denishawn Magazine	†																			
321 Greenwich Playbill	†	*																		
322 Jewish Theatrical News	†	*																		

1925-1944 *(cont.)*

No.	Title	1925	1926	1927	1928	1929	1930	1931	1932	1933	1934	1935	1936	1937	1938	1939	1940	1941	1942	1943	1944
323	Little Theatrical Monthly	†	*																		
324	Little Theatre News	†																			
325	Little Theatre Play List	†																			
327	N.Y. Amusements	†	*	*	*	*	*	*	*	*	*	*	*	*	*						
328	Players Magazine	†	*	*	*	*	*	*	*	*	*	*	*	*	*	*	*	*	*	*	†
329	Shakespeare Assoc. Bull.	†	*	*	*	*	*	*	*	*	*	*	*	*	*	*	*	*	*	*	†
331	Actors Directory	*	*																		
332	Continental Theatre	*	*																		
334	N.Y. The. Bus. Men's G.	*	*	*																	
335	Pasadena Com. Playhouse	*	*	*	*	*	*	*	*	*	*	*	*	*	*	*	*	*	*	*	†
336	Playbill	*	*	*	*	*	*	*	*	*	*	*	*	*	*	*	*	*	*	*	†
337	Professional Bull.	*	*																		
339	Repertory Spectator	*	*																		
340	Show World	*	*	*	*																
342	Stage & Screen	*	*																		
343	TPROA Quill	*	*	*	*	*	*	*	*	*											
344	Playgoer		*	*	*	*	*	*	*	*	*	*	*	*	*	*	*	*	*	*	†
345	American Dancer			*	*	*	*	*	*	*	*	*	*	*	*	*	*	*	*		
346	Church & Drama Bulletin				*	*	*	*	*												
347	Journal of Expression				*	*	*	*	*	*											
348	Little Theatre of Dallas				*	*	*	*	*	*	*	*	*	*	*	*	*	*	*	*	
349	Log of Little Theatre				*	*	*	*	*	*	*	*	*	*	*	*	*	*	*	*	†
350	Scenic Artist				*	*															
353	Carolina Play-Book					*	*	*	*	*	*	*	*	*	*	*	*	*	*	*	*
354	Footlights & Kliegs					*	*														
357	Theatre News						*	*	*	*											
358	Circus Scrap Book						*	*	*	*											
359	Drama Service Bull.						*	*													
360	Harlequinade						*	*													
361	High School Thespian						*	*	*	*	*	*	*	*	*	*	*	*	*	*	†
363	Playbill							*	*	*	*	*	*	*	*	*	*	*	*	*	†
364	Rob Wagner's Script							*	*	*	*	*	*	*	*	*	*	*	*	*	†
368	Civic Repertory							*	*												
369	Dancers Club News							*	*	*											
370	Olympian							*	*	*	*	*									
371	Prompter Mount Vernon							*	*	*	*										
372	Puppetry							*	*	*	*	*	*	*	*	*	*	*	*	*	†
373	Shakespeare Studies							*	*	*											
374	Theatre Engineering							*	*												
375	Call Board								*	*	*	*	*	*	*	*	*	*	*	*	†
376	Lagniappe								*	*	*	*	*	*	*	*	*	*	*	*	†
377	Practical Stage Work								*	*	*										
379	Seven Circles								*	*	*	*									
380	Silver Falcon								*	*	*	*	*	*							
382	Worker's Theatre								*	*	*										
384	Cue									*	*	*	*	*	*	*	*	*	*	*	†
385	Dragon									*	*	*	*	*	*	*	*	*	*	*	†
386	Lambs Script									*	*	*	*	*	*	*	*	*	*	*	†
391	Iowa Play Production									*	*	*	*	*	*	*	*	*	*	*	†
392	Little Theatres									*	*	*	*								
394	Playhouse										*	*	*								
395	Four Arts										*	*									
396	Jinx										*	*	*	*	*	*	*	*			

1925-1944 *(cont.)*

	1925	1926	1927	1928	1929	1930	1931	1932	1933	1934	1935	1936	1937	1938	1939	1940	1941	1942	1943	1944
397 New Theatre										*	*	*	*							
398 Am. Gilbert & Sullivan											*	*	*	*						
399 Aria											*	*	*							
400 Charles T. Jordan											*	*								
401 Federal Theatre											*	*	*	*						
402 Handy Green Book											*	*	*	*	*	*				
404 Theatre News											*	*	*	*	*	*				
405 Carolina Stage												*	*	*	*	*	*	*	*	*
406 Centre Aisle												*	*	*	*	*	*	*	*	
407 Drama												*	*	*						
409 Little Theatre News												*	*	*						
411 Opera News												*	*	*	*	*	*	*	*	†
412 Theatre Workshop												*	*	*						
413 Tops												*	*	*	*	*	*	*		†
414 Arts Quarterly													*	*	*					
415 Catholic Theatre Conf.													*	*	*	*	*	*		†
417 Grapevine Telegraph													*	*	*	*	*	*		†
419 One Act Play Mag.													*	*	*	*	*	*		
421 Bull. Drama. Assembly														*	*	*	*	*		†
422 Catholic The. Year Book														*	*	*	*	*		
423 C. Brown's The. Rec.														*	*					
425 Continental Theatre														*	*					
426 Curtain Rises														*	*	*				
427 Dramatis Personae														*	*					
428 Negro Actor														*	*	*				
429 New Theatre News														*	*	*	*			
430 Non-profess. Drama														*	*					
431 Play Shop														*	*	*	*	*	*	†
433 Scene														*	*	*				
434 School & Theatre														*	*					
435 Stage Practice														*	*	*	*	*		
436 TAC														*	*	*				
437 The. Lib. Assoc. Rep.														*	*	*	*	*	*	
441 Comm. The. Cue															*	*	*	*	*	
442 Drama Educators of Am.															*	*	*			
444 Info about New York															*	*				
445 Little The. Sou. Calif.															*	*	*	*		
446 Luntanne Tatler															*	*				
448 Nat. The. Conference															*	*	*	*	*	†
449 News-letter															*	*	*	*	*	†
450 Theatre Arts Signpost															*	*	*			
453 Asides																*	*	*	*	†
454 Broadside																*	*	*	*	†
455 Conjurer's Chatter																*	*	*	*	†
456 Critics' The. Reviews																*	*	*	*	†
458 Drama Leaguer																*	*	*	*	
461 Negro Actors Guild																*	*	*	*	
462 Opera																*	*			
464 Short Hauls																*	*	*	*	†
465 Stage																*	*			
467 AETA News																	*	*	*	†
468 Actor's Cue																	*	*	*	†
470 Bandwagon																	*	*	*	†

1925-1944 *(cont.)*

No.	Title	1941	1942	1943	1944
471	Border Light	*	*		
472	Directory of Music	*	*	*	†
475	Lest We Forget	*	*	*	†
476	Plays	*	*	*	†
478	Show Business	*	*	*	†
479	Straw Hats	*	*		
481	Catholic Theatergoer		*	*	†
482	Dramatic Center News		*	*	†
483	Theatre Annual		*	*	†
484	Hugard's Magic Monthly			*	†
485	Teater Heftn			*	†
486	Theatre Book			*	†
487	Two Masques			*	*
490	Players Guide				†
491	Stage Pictorial				†
492	Theatrical Calendar				†
493	Univ. of Wash. Pub.				†

1945-1964

No.	Title	1945	1946	1947	1948	1949	1950	1951	1952	1953	1954	1955	1956	1957	1958	1959	1960	1961	1962	1963	1964
109	Poet Lore	†	*	*	*	*	*	*	*	*											
120	Billboard	†	*	*	*	*	*	*	*	*	*	*	*	*	*	*	*	*			
142	Cast	†	*	*	*	*	*	*	*	*	*										
162	Sphinx	†	*	*	*	*	*														
184	Variety	†	*	*	*	*	*	*	*	*	*	*	*	*	*	*	*	*	*	*	†
267	Equity	†	*	*	*	*	*	*	*	*	*	*	*	*	*	*	*	*	*	*	†
276	Theatre Arts	†	*	*	*	*	*	*	*	*	*	*	*	*	*	*	*	*	*	*	*
302	Cue	†	*	*	*	*	*	*	*	*	*	*	*	*	*	*	*				
328	Players Magazine	†	*	*	*	*	*	*	*	*	*	*	*	*	*	*	*	*	*	*	†
329	Shakespeare Assoc. Bull.	†	*	*	*	*															
335	Pasadena Com. Playhouse	†	*	*																	
336	Playbill	†	*	*	*	*	*	*	*	*	*	*	*	*	*	*	*	*	*	*	†
344	Playgoer	†	*	*	*	*	*	*	*	*											
349	Log of Little Theatre	†	*	*	*	*	*	*	*	*	*	*	*	*	*	*	*	*	*	*	†
361	High School Thespian	†	*	*	*	*	*	*	*	*	*	*	*	*	*	*	*	*	*	*	†
363	Playbill	†	*	*	*	*	*	*	*	*	*	*	*	*	*	*	*	*	*	*	†
364	Rob Wagner's Script	†	*	*	*	*															
372	Puppetry	†	*	*																	
375	Call Board	†	*	*	*	*	*	*	*	*	*	*	*	*	*	*	*	*	*	*	†
376	Lagniappe	†	*	*	*	*	*	*	*	*	*	*	*	*	*	*	*	*	*		
384	Cue	†	*	*	*	*	*	*	*	*	*	*	*	*	*	*	*	*	*	*	†
385	Dragon	†	*																		
386	Lambs Script	†	*	*	*	*	*	*	*	*	*	*	*	*	*	*	*	*			
391	Iowa Play Production	†	*	*	*	*	*	*	*	*											
411	Opera News	†	*	*	*	*	*	*	*	*	*	*	*	*	*	*	*	*	*	*	†
413	Tops	†	*	*	*	*	*	*	*	*	*	*									
415	Catholic Theatre Conf.	†	*	*	*	*	*	*	*	*	*	*	*	*	*	*	*	*	*	*	†
417	Grapevine Telegraph	†	*	*	*																
421	Bull. Drama. Assembly	†	*	*	*																
431	Play Shop	†	*	*	*	*	*	*													
448	Nat. The. Conference	†	*	*	*	*	*														
449	News-letter	†	*	*	*																

1945-1964 *(cont.)*

	1945	1946	1947	1948	1949	1950	1951	1952	1953	1954	1955	1956	1957	1958	1959	1960	1961	1962	1963	1964
453 Asides	†	*	*	*																
454 Broadside	†	*	*	*	*	*	*	*	*	*	*	*	*	*	*	*	*	*	*	
455 Conjurer's Chatter	†	*	*																	
456 Critics' The. Reviews	†	*	*	*	*	*	*	*	*	*	*	*	*	*	*	*	*	*	*	†
464 Short Hauls													*							
467 AETA News	†	*	*	*	*															
468 Actor's Cue	†	*	*	*																
470 Bandwagon	†	*	*																	
472 Directory of Music	†	*	*	*	*	*	*	*	*	*	*	*	*	*	*	*	*	*	*	†
475 Lest We Forget	†	*	*	*	*	*	*	*	*											
476 Plays	†	*	*	*	*	*	*	*	*	*	*	*	*	*	*	*	*	*	*	†
478 Show Business	†	*	*	*	*	*	*	*	*	*	*	*	*	*	*	*	*	*	*	*
481 Catholic Theatregoer	†	*	*	*	*	*	*	*	*	*	*									
482 Dramatic Center News	†	*	*	*	*	*	*	*	*	*	*	*	*	*	*	*	*	*	*	†
483 Theatre Annual	†	*	*	*	*	*	*	*	*	*	*	*	*	*	*	*	*	*	*	†
484 Hugard's Magic Monthly	†	*	*	*	*	*	*	*	*	*	*	*	*	*	*	*	*			
485 Teater Heftn	†	*	*																	
486 Theatre Book	†	*	*	*	*	*														
490 Players Guide	†	*	*	*	*	*	*	*	*	*	*	*	*	*	*	*	*	*	*	†
491 Stage Pictorial	†	*	*																	
492 Theatrical Calendar	†	*	*																	
493 Univ. of Wash. Pub.	†																			
494 New Conjurors' Magazine	*	*	*	*																
495 Notes on Am. Theatre	*	*																		
496 Prologue	*	*	*	*	*	*	*	*	*	*	*	*	*	*	*	*	*	*	*	†
497 Theatre World	*	*	*	*	*	*	*	*	*	*	*	*	*	*	*	*	*	*	*	†
498 Am. Repertory Theatre	*	*																		
499 Bandwagon	*	*	*	*	*	*	*	*	*	*	*	*	*	*	*	*	*	*	*†	
501 Hobby-Swapper	*	*	*	*	*	*														
504 Pacific Theatre	*	*																		
506 Talent Review					*	*	*	*												
508 Curtain Call					*	*	*	*	*	*	*	*	*							
510 Prologue & Epilogue					*	*														
511 Prompt Box					*	*	*	*	*	*	*									
513 Theatre Craft					*	*														
514 Wisconsin Idea Theatre					*	*	*	*	*	*	*	*								
515 Chrysalis						*	*	*	*	*	*	*	*	*	*	*	*			
516 Footnotes						*	*	*	*	*	*	*	*	*	*	*	*	*	*	†
517 Poetry Book Magazine						*	*	*	*	*	*	*	*	*	*	*	*	*	*	†
522 Broadway Sign Post						*	*	*	*											
523 Bull. of Comediantes							*	*	*	*	*	*	*	*	*	*	*	*	*	†
525 Educational The. Journal							*	*	*	*	*	*	*	*	*	*	*	*	*	†
526 Puppetry Journal							*	*	*	*	*	*	*	*	*	*	*	*	*	*
528 Theatre Time Magazine							*	*	*	*										
529 AGVA News								*	*	*	*	*	*	*	*	*	*	*	*	†
530 ANTA News								*	*	*	*	*	*							
531 Dancing Star								*	*	*	*	*	*	*	*	*	*			
532 Folk Dance Federation								*	*	*	*	*	*	*	*	*	*	*	*	†
533 Magicol								*	*	*										
534 Shakespeare Quarterly								*	*	*	*	*	*	*	*	*	*	*	*	†
535 Stanford Players News.							*	*	*	*										
536 Summer Theatres							*	*	*	*	*	*	*	*	*	*	*	*	*	†
537 Theatre News Weekly							*	*												

1945-1964 *(cont.)*

	1945	1946	1947	1948	1949	1950	1951	1952	1953	1954	1955	1956	1957	1958	1959	1960	1961	1962	1963	1964
538 AETA Directory							*	*	*	*	*	*	*	*	*	*	*	*	*	†
539 Critical Digest							*	*	*	*	*	*	*	*	*	*	*	*	*	†
540 International Theatre							*		*											
544 Shakespeare Newsletter							*	*	*	*	*	*	*	*	*	*	*	*	*	†
545 Shaw Society of Am.							*	*	*	*	*	*	*	*	*	*	*	*	*	†
546 Southwest Theatre Conf.							*	*												
547 Who's Where							*	*	*	*	*	*	*	*	*	*	*			
548 Curtain Time								*	*	*	*	*	*	*	*	*	*	*	*	†
549 Pasadena Playhouse								*	*	*	*	*	*	*	*	*	*	*		
550 Greek Theatre Magazine								*	*	*	*	*	*	*	*	*	*	*	*	†
551 Theatre							*	*	*	*										
553 Center							*	*	*											
554 Central Opera Service							*	*	*	*	*	*	*	*	*	*	*	*	*	†
555 Chapter One							*	*	*	*	*	*	*	*	*	*	*	*	*	†
556 Educational The. News							*	*	*	*	*	*	*	*	*	*	*	*	*	†
557 Lyric Opera Program											*	*	*	*	*	*	*	*	*	†
559 OSU The. Coll. Bull.											*	*	*	*	*	*	*	*	*	†
560 Opera Annual											*	*	*	*	*	*	*	*	*	†
562 Stubs											*	*	*	*	*		*			
563 The. Arts News Service											*	*	*							
565 Yale Drama Alumni News.									*	*	*	*	*	*	*					
566 ANTA Newsletter										*	*	*	*	*	*	*	*	*		
567 Carleton Drama Review										*	*	*	*	*	*	*	*	*	*	†
568 Community The. Bull.										*	*	*	*	*	*					
569 Harlequin										*	*	*	*	*						
571 NJTL Bulletin										*	*	*	*	*	*	*	*	*	*	†
572 Playhouse Reporter										*	*	*	*							
574 Simon's Directory										*	*	*	*	*	*	*	*	*	*	†
575 Actors Forum											*	*								
576 Alice Gerstenberg											*	*	*							
577 Am. National Theatre											*	*	*	*	*	*	*	*		
578 Catholic Preview											*	*	*							
580 Inter. Theatre Annual											*	*	*	*						
581 Lyric Opera News											*	*	*	*	*	*	*	*	*	†
582 NOA Newsletter											*	*	*	*	*	*	*	*	*	†
583 Performing Arts											*	*	*	*	*	*				
584 Shaw Society Newsletter											*	*	*	*	*	*	*	*	*	†
585 Southern Theatre News											*	*	*	*	*	*	*	*	*	*
587 ASTR Newsletter												*	*	*	*	*	*	*	*	†
589 Broadway's Best												*	*	*	*					
591 Funspot													*	*	*	*				
592 Guide to Perf. Arts													*	*	*	*	*	*	*	†
593 Playbill														*	*	*	*	*	*	†
595 ANTA-LA Newsletter															*	*	*	*	*	†
596 ANTA Spotlight															*	*	*	*	*	
597 Chorus														*	*	*	*	*	*	†
598 Critique														*	*	*	*	*	*	†
600 Harlequin														*	*					
601 Modern Drama														*	*	*	*	*	*	†
602 On Stage														*	*					
606 Children's The. Conf.																*	*	*	*	
607 Children's The. Res.																*	*			
608 Dance Perspectives																*	*	*	*	†

1945-1964 *(cont.)*

	1959	1960	1961	1962	1963	1964
610 Prog. of Met. Opera	*	*	*	*	*	†
612 Theatre	*	*	*	*		
617 Am. Little The. Mag.			*	*		
618 Back Stage			*	*		
619 Billboard Overseas		*	*	*	*	†
621 California Shavian		*	*	*	*	†
622 Charles Playbook		*	*	*	*	†
623 Coward-McCann Drama		*	*	*	*	†
624 Dramatists' Bulletin		*	*	*	*	*
626 8:30 Theatre		*	*	*		
627 En'core	*	*	*	*	†	
628 N.Y. State Com. The.	*	*	*	*	†	
630 Stratford Studies	*	*	*	*	†	
631 Theatre & Events	*	*	*	*	†	
632 Theatre Survey	*	*	*	*	†	
634 Amusement Business			*	*	*	†
635 Curtain Call			*	*	*	†
636 Drama Survey			*	*	*	†
637 First Stage			*	*	*	†
638 Impressario			*	*	*	†
639 Leaguer			*	*	*	†
641 Show			*	*	*	†
642 Show Business Illus.			*	*		
644 Dance-Music-Drama				*	*	†
645 Dunster Drama Review				*	*	*
646 Footlight				*	*	†
647 Independent Shavians				*	*	†
648 Musical Show				*	*	†
649 Playbill				*	*	†
651 Script				*	*	†
652 17th & 18th C. The.				*	*	†
653 Southern Sawdust				*	*	†
655 ANTA News Bulletin					*	†
656 Harvard Drama Review					*	*
659 Ante						†
660 Curtain Playwrights						†
661 Dance Year						†
662 Dramatists Guild Quart.						†
663 Folk Music Yearbook						†
664 Lincoln Center						†
665 Players Showcase						†
667 Religious Theatre						†
669 Setting the Stage						†
671 Theatre						†

1965-1968

	1965	1966	1967	1968
184 Variety	†	*	*	*
267 Equity	†	*	*	*
328 Players Magazine	†	*	*	*
336 Playbill	†	*	*	*
349 Log of Little Theatre	†	*	*	*

1965-1967 *(cont.)*	1965	1966	1967	1968
361 High School Thespian	†	*	*	*
363 Playbill	†	*	*	*
375 Call Board	†	*	*	*
384 Cue	†	*	*	*
411 Opera News	†	*	*	*
415 Catholic Theatre Conf.	†	*	*	*
456 Critics' The. Reviews	†	*	*	*
472 Directory of Music	†	*	*	*
476 Plays	†	*	*	*
482 Dramatic Center News	†	*		
490 Players Guide	†	*	*	*
496 Prologue	†	*	*	*
497 Theatre World	†	*	*	*
499 Bandwagon	†	*	*	*
516 Footnotes	†	*	*	*
517 Poetry Book Magazine	†	*	*	*
523 Bull. of Comediantes	†	*	*	*
525 Educational The. Journal	†	*	*	*
529 AGVA News	†	*	*	*
532 Folk Dance Federation	†	*	*	*
534 Shakespeare Quarterly	†	*	*	*
536 Summer Theatres	†	*	*	*
538 AETA Directory	†	*	*	*
539 Critical Digest	†	*	*	*
544 Shakespeare Newsletter	†	*	*	*
545 Shaw Society of Am.	†	*	*	*
548 Curtain Time	†	*	*	*
550 Greek Theatre Magazine	†	*	*	*
554 Central Opera Service	†	*	*	*
555 Chapter One	†			
556 Educational The. News	†	*	*	*
557 Lyric Opera Program	†	*	*	*
559 OSU The. Coll. Bull.	†	*	*	*
560 Opera Annual	†	*	*	*
567 Carleton Drama Review	†	*	*	*
571 NJTL Bulletin	†	*	*	*
574 Simon's Directory	†	*	*	*
581 Lyric Opera News	†	*	*	*
582 NOA Newsletter	†	*	*	*
584 Shaw Society Newsletter	†	*	*	*
587 ASTR Newsletter	†	*	*	*
592 Guide to Perf. Arts	†	*	*	*
593 Playbill	†	*	*	*
595 ANTA-LA Newsletter	†	*	*	*
597 Chorus	†	*	*	*
598 Critique	†	*	*	*
601 Modern Drama	†	*	*	*
608 Dance Perspectives	†	*	*	*
610 Prog. of Met. Opera	†	*	*	*
619 Billboard Overseas	†	*	*	*
621 California Shavian	†	*	*	*
623 Coward-McCann Drama	†	*	*	*
627 En'core	†			

	1965	1966	1967	1968
1965-1967 *(cont.)*				
628 N.Y. State Com. The.	†	*	*	*
630 Stratford Studies	†	*	*	*
631 Theatre & Events	†	*	*	*
632 Theatre Survey	†	*	*	*
634 Amusement Business	†	*	*	*
635 Curtain Call	†	*	*	*
636 Drama Survey	†	*	*	*
637 First Stage	†	*	*	*
638 Impressario	†	*	*	*
639 Leaguer	†	*	*	*
641 Show	†			
644 Dance-Music-Drama	†	*	*	*
646 Footlight	†	*	*	*
647 Independent Shavians	†	*	*	*
648 Musical Show	†	*	*	*
649 Playbill	†	*	*	*
651 Script	†	*	*	*
652 17th & 18th C. The.	†	*	*	*
653 Southern Sawdust	†	*	*	
655 ANTA News Bulletin	†	*	*	*
659 Ante	†	*	*	*
660 Curtain Playwrights	†	*	*	*
661 Dance Year	†	*	*	*
662 Dramatists Guild Quart.	†	*	*	*
663 Folk Music Yearbook	†	*	*	*
664 Lincoln Center	†	*	*	*
665 Players Showcase	†			
667 Religious Theatre	†	*	*	*
669 Setting the Stage	†	*	*	*
671 Theatre	†	*	*	*
672 Afro-Asian The. Bull.	*	*	*	*
677 SRO	*	*	*	*
678 Shakespeare Studies	*	*	*	*
679 Theatre Design & Tech.	*	*	*	*
680 Opera Co. of Boston		*	*	*
681 Something Else		*	*	*
682 Comparative Drama			*	*
684 Modern Inter. Drama			*	*
685 Theatre Crafts			*	*

Index

*All initial definite and indefinite articles are omitted from the titles of the periodicals.